Glories of the Vegetarian Table

Glories of the Vegetarian Table

A Collection of Contemporary Vegetarian Recipes & Menus

Janet Hazen

Aris Books

▲ Addison-Wesley Publishing Company, Inc.

Reading, Massachusetts   Menlo Park, California   New York
Don Mills, Ontario   Wokingham, England   Amsterdam   Bonn
Sydney   Singapore   Tokyo   Madrid   San Juan

Copyright © 1988 by Janet Hazen

Library of Congress Cataloging-in-Publication Data
Hazen, Janet.
  Glories of the vegetarian table: a collection of contemporary vegetarian recipes and menus / Janet Hazen.
    p.   cm.—(Kitchen edition)
    Includes index.
    ISBN 0-201-12631-1
    1. Vegetarian cookery.   I. Title.   II. Series.
  TX837.H42 1988
  641.5′636—dc19   88-29413
                                                        CIP

Kitchen Edition books are published by Aris Books,
an imprint of Addison-Wesley Publishing Company, Inc.

Aris Books Editorial Offices and Test Kitchen
1621 Fifth Street
Berkeley, CA 94710
(415) 527-5171

Series Editor: John Harris
Project Editor: Lee Mooney
Consulting Editor: S. Irene Virbila
Series Design: Lynne O'Neil
Cover Photo: Lisa Blevins
Cover Design: Copenhaver Cumpston
Food Stylist: Stevie Bass
Illustrations: Pamela Manley
Set in 10 point Baskerville by Another Point, Inc., Oakland, CA

ABCDEFGHIJ—DO—898
First Printing, November 1988

Contents

Dedication—
For Herb, Irene and Bruce

Acknowledgments

I would like to thank Steve and Lisa Vance for their constant and cheerful support, help and handholding. These computer wizards eased my phobia and turned me into a wimpy but semiconfident computer person. Without their help, this project would have been a nightmare!

Many thanks to Judy Blundell for technical and emotional counseling. Starting *anything* in life would be difficult without her insight and support.

Introduction

Okay. I'll come clean from the start. I am not a vegetarian. Sure, I *used* to be, back when for me food and eating were not all-encompassing . . . a guiding light . . . a way of life . . . a consuming passion . . . a driving force. In those days vegetarians ate vegetables. Maybe they ate the popular beans-and-rice combo, cheese, perhaps eggs, depending on the type of vegetarian they were, and plenty of fruits and nuts. Eventually vegetarian eating changed. "Grains" began to appear everywhere, followed by tofu, not to mention all varieties of soy substitutes and other strange and foreign food substances. Just about that time crisp, golden, smoky, and irresistibly delicious bacon found its way into my mouth. I know, of all things—bacon. But it was time.

An ever-increasing awareness of food and how it affects the body and mind has opened the eyes of many people. The current trend in diets is low-fat, high-carbohydrate, and low-protein, which results in lighter food in general. Many people are turning to vegetarian menus for this reason. Gone are the days of soggy vegetable stews laden with undigestible, half-cooked mystery beans and topped with rubbery cheese. Granted, not all 1960s vegetarian dishes fall into this category, but enough do . . . just enough to scare off the unadventurous, close-minded or traditional meat-and-potato eaters! Luckily, there are new ideas in vegetarian eating. Those scarred and wounded from the prehistoric vegetarian battles of yesteryear have exciting new options.

Meatless dining can be extremely rewarding and fulfilling, sometimes more than traditional dining. I have no religous, spiritual, political or nutritional directives to offer here. The recipes are original and reliable, written with passion and dedication. Herein lie many delectable, creative and unique ideas and recipes ripe for the picking.

It is not enough to simply "omit the meat, poultry, fish or seafood" when cooking vegetarian meals. One must become sensitive to the qualities of individual foods and how they react and combine with one another. Vegetarian cooking is not mysterious or complicated, but it does require a discerning touch and a willingness to create new masterpieces in novel ways.

The dishes in this book are designed for vegetarians as well as nonvegetarians. Each recipe incorporates individual ingredients that sing on their own and have true merit whether they are combined with meat, poultry, seafood, dairy or vegetables. This book is dedicated to those passionate about life, who love to eat, drink and entertain. The menus are satisfying, complete and full of varied foodstuffs, guaranteed to please fussy eaters, jaded palates and even confirmed carnivores.

Presentation is very important to me. We all like to eat good food, prepared with love and attention, sometimes even in abundant proportions. Why not make the plates beautiful and pleasing to the eye at the same time? Eating can be the inhalation of food out-of-hand over the sink, which I do from time to time. Or it can be a jovial, sensuous, memorable experience, rich with stimulating conversation, good wine and fabulous food . . . an occasion to be remembered by all.

When I cook for my friends and family, the food is usually interesting, plentiful and attractive. Second and sometimes even third helpings are asked for. Wine and wit are abundant, conversation is relaxing and stimulating— the important things are taken care of. But then there is the table. We usually dine amid books, papers, bowls of fruit and telephone wires, not to mention a copious number of phone calls. My friends are used to it. They say they can't eat the table anyway. Well, what I'm getting at is that some things can slide, but the food must taste and look good.

This book is divided into smaller courses so that menus can be developed with ease. There are some sample menus at the end of the book, organized by themes. Some feature a certain food type, for instance, corn, eggplant, or onions, leeks and garlic; others are designed around holidays when food is central to the celebration.

Most of the recipes yield six to eight servings, but as we know, serving size is a personal matter! You can pretty much rely on six or seven people eating and feeling good at the end of each meal prepared from this book.

Outlined in the Basics chapter are some guidelines for successful vegetarian cooking. The first sentence of the ingredients section of that chapter states an idea I cannot stress enough: "It is essential to use quality ingredients." Think back on the times when you sunk your teeth into a ripe, sweet, red tomato bursting with juice and flavor, or a tart green apple, crisp, firm and exploding with goodness. Compare these heavenly moments of culinary history to the sad and pathetic mouthfuls of mediocre food, mouthfuls taken out of sheer hunger or simply out of necessity. Good food makes good food, period. Also please read about basic equipment, techniques and tips, all of which will help you cook from this book.

I would like to make one final suggestion. Make the snack on page 10 or any other snack before you sit down to read this book. It is important to understand certain concepts and basic techniques before using the recipes. But, *do* have a snack to ward off the hunger demons while you peruse the opening chapters. Nothing is worse than trying to read about food on an empty stomach.

Cooking and preparing food is a glorious process, and it pleases me greatly to share my ideas and recipes with fellow cooks. I hope this book brings many enjoyable and rewarding meals to your table.

Snack

6 thin slices sharp
 Vermont or Canadian
 Cheddar cheese
2 thick slices fresh
 whole wheat bread
3 to 4 cornichons, sliced
 thin
1 thin slice red onion
2 fresh tomato slices
2 to 3 Tb. unsalted
 butter

Make a sandwich by placing 3 slices of the cheese on one piece of the bread, arrange the cornichons, red onion and the tomatoes on top of the cheese, top with remaining cheese and second piece of bread. Press the sandwich to secure the ingredients. Melt half the butter in a small skillet. Place sandwich in pan and cook, over low heat, covered, until one side is golden brown. Add the remaining butter to the pan and melt. Gently flip the sandwich and cook on reverse side until the bread is golden brown and the cheese is melted. You may find it helpful to cover the skillet with a lid; this helps the cheese to melt without browning the bread too much. Eat this toasty delight with anything you want, but make sure you have a frosty beer in one hand.

Basics

Basic Ingredients

It is essential to use quality ingredients. The final masterpiece can only be as good as the ingredients used along the way. Passion and devotion are not a replacement for mediocre products! With this in mind, read on and feel free to indulge in the finest olive oils, aromatic vinegars and new and exotic herbs and spices. Enjoy each season's bounty of fresh, healthy and stimulating fruits and vegetables.

Butter

Use only unsalted or "sweet" butter for cooking. Unsalted butter is fresher, tastes 100 percent better than salted butter and it allows you to control the salt content of your food. Why insist on using unsalted butter and then adding salt to the food anyway? Good question. Not only do you have more control, you have a choice. If no additional salt is needed, then don't add any! If the food does call for salt, then add what you must. Remember, cultivating a taste for salt isn't such a great idea anyway.

Doughs

Filo dough is a type of unyeasted Middle Eastern dough. It is paper thin and very delicate. Filo dough can be found in the frozen-food section of most supermarkets, specialty food stores and Middle Eastern stores. It must be thawed before using, and then covered with a damp towel to prevent drying.

Rice paper is used for Imperial Rolls (see page 46). This is a very thin, brittle "wrapper" used in many Southeast Asian dishes. The round sheets are dried on bamboo mats, which creates a cross-hatch pattern on the surface of each sheet. Brushing or spraying the rice papers with water makes them pliable and soft. They must be covered at all times with a damp cloth to prevent additional drying.

Flavoring Agents and Condiments

By flavoring agents I mean prepared liquids, pastes and sauces that accent, highlight or help pull the flavor out of the pot and into your mouth. These bottles, jars and cans of magic may appear to be all too common or even old hat, but in the hands of a creative cook, they really show off their powers. If you're already a believer in "a drop of this" or "a pinch of that," then you already understand the basic idea.

A few basic flavoring agents are essential: soy sauce, mushroom soy sauce, teriyaki, Angostura bitters and hot pepper sauce or Tabasco sauce. An assortment of mustards is useful as well. A combination of two or three mustards can be outstanding in many recipes. Choose four basic prepared mustards for your pantry: French-style Dijon, Chinese hot, German-style sweet and a coarse-grain mustard. Prepared horseradish and Japanese wasabi (a pungent green horseradish made from a root) are good to have around. Capers or green peppercorns in brine, sun-dried tomatoes, tahini, sesame paste, miso (red or white), honey and maple syrup are other ingredients used in this book.

For the most part these are readily available in any market, natural-food store or specialty shop. Nowadays, even major supermarket chains have ethnic food departments that include some of the basic ingredients for Chinese, Japanese, Southeast Asian, Latin and Italian cooking.

Herbs and Spices

Following are a few basic guidelines for the purchasing, storage and use of herbs and spices.

Herbs are the leaves of certain plants and trees that grow in moderate climates. Spices are the buds, seeds, fruits, flowers, bark and roots of plants and trees, many of which grow in hot tropical climates.

When buying fresh herbs look for lively, young green herbs, with leaves intact and stems unbruised. Store fresh herbs in a sealed plastic bag, or submerge the roots in a small container of water and cover with a plastic bag. Dry herbs should be fresh in a different way—full of flavor and heady with their perfume. Store dry herbs in a cool, dark place. I have seen so many kitchens where the dry herbs are stored just above the stove area—there couldn't be a place more damaging for herbs than that! The intense and constant heat destroys the oils in the herbs, which contain most of the flavor.

When a recipe in this book calls for mixed herbs and does not specify dry herbs, use a combination of these fresh herbs: chives, curly leaf parsley, marjoram, oregano and thyme. Personally, I like to go heavy on chives and lighter on oregano, but you will have your own preference.

Herbs and spices are used to accentuate, perk up or add dimension to food, not to mask or compete with the natural flavors. Become familiar with a variety of herbs and spices. Rub the leaves between your fingers and inhale their perfume. Taste them. Use new herbs or spices with a light hand until you really know the effect they have on foods. Remember, you can always add more at the end, but you can't take out what you already put in.

Generally speaking, add dry herbs and spices at the beginning of the cooking process so that they have time to release their flavors and blend with the food. Heat "wears down" fresh herbs and spices. Add fresh herbs at the end of cooking, just before the dish is done.

Most of the spices in these recipes are called for in their whole form, for example, whole allspice instead of ground allspice, cardamom pods instead of ground carda-mom. When black pepper is called for, use freshly ground black peppercorns. I strongly urge you to grind your own spices. Whole spices stay fresher longer than ground spices, and home-grinding is fun anyway. When a recipe calls for a spice in its whole form, measure it in that form, then grind it and add to the other ingredients.

Oils

Nut Oils—Some wonderful nut oils are available these days. Most frequently called for in this book are walnut, hazelnut and sesame (which is actually a seed, not a nut). Pecan and almond oils have their place, as well as peanut oil, which is used in most Asian cooking. Freshness and high quality are essential properties to look for when purchasing nut oils. Refrigerate after opening because, like other natural oils, nut oils can become rancid in a warm kitchen.

Olive Oil—Select olive oils that are cold-pressed, which means that the oils were extracted without heat, water or chemicals. *Extra virgin* olive oil is made from the first pressing of the best olives, *virgin* is usually made from the subsequent pressings of lesser quality olives and *pure* olive oil is most often made from remaining pulp, skins and pits. Pure olive oil is the least flavorful. Choose pale green, fruity oils when the flavor of the oil is the star or a main flavor in the recipe. Use golden, sweeter, less assertive oils for subtle vinaigrettes and most cooking. Olive oil has a relatively low smoking point and should not be used in place of vegetable oils for frying.

Vegetable Oils—Have on hand at least one vegetable oil such as safflower, soybean, corn oil or a generic vegetable oil. Safflower, soybean, cottonseed, grapeseed and corn oil have relatively high smoking points, so use one of these for frying. You won't want to use vegetable oils for making vinaigrettes because they have very little taste— an advantage when frying foods.

Vinegars

I always have six or seven vinegars on hand. My list of basic vinegars includes: balsamic, white wine, red wine, champagne, apple cider, sherry and rice wine (seasoned and unseasoned). Some nice additions are: black rice, blackberry, raspberry, blueberry, kiwi, peach, pear, cherry, and assorted citrus fruit, herb and spice vinegars. When buying vinegar, look for unpasteurized, chemical-free varieties.

Wine and Distilled Liquids

At the risk of repeating something you may already know, I will simply say: In cooking, use only wines that you would happily drink out of glass. If a recipe calls for red wine, choose a dry, full-bodied Zinfandel, Cabernet Sauvignon, Merlot or Burgundy. These wines retain their flavor and body through the cooking process. White wines should be dry as well. Sauvignon Blanc, Chardonnay or a good dry table wine will work well. You needn't spend an entire pay check on cooking wines, unless, of course, you can. More often than not you can find suitable cooking wines in the four- to seven-dollar range. Invest in good bottles of dry sherry, Madeira, port and brandy. Their unique flavors are indispensable in many recipes.

Basic Equipment

A well-equipped kitchen is a delight to work in. To be caught in the middle of a project without the necessary tools is frustrating, to say the least. Most cooking can be done with basic, good-quality cookware.

The recipes in this book require a few standard pieces of equipment. Naturally I want you to purchase within your budget, but remember, quality products have longer lives and will definitely add to your enjoyment in the kitchen.

Basically, if you cook at all you will already have all the required equipment. Vegetarian cooking doesn't require any special gadgets or expensive exotic pots and pans, just good solid cookware.

Knives

The cook's most valuable tool is the knife. Whether you choose carbon steel, stainless steel or high-carbon stainless steel knives, the important thing is that you respect your knives and keep them clean and sharp. As far as I'm concerned, trying to cut anything with a dull knife is a step closer to a day in hell.

For easy prepping, you'll need three knives: a paring knife, a long serrated knife and a good solid French or chef's knife, 8-inch, 10-inch or 12-inch, whichever size you feel most comfortable using. You may also want to have a Japanese vegetable knife, which is smaller and lighter and has a thinner blade than most French knives. With these three or four basic knives you can cut anything and everything called for in this book.

Pots and Pans

For top-of-the-stove cooking you will need a large 10- to 12-gallon stockpot, assorted saucepans and pots, and some sort of steamer. Your usual cookware is probably just fine. If you are going out to buy some new pots and pans, be sure to look for heavy-bottomed, heavy-gauge ones, preferably with nonstick surfaces.

Bakeware

Baking cookware includes heavy-gauge sheet pans, a couple of baking pans, pie pans, a loaf or bread pan, and 1-cup timbale molds or deep cupcake pans.

Machines

A spice grinder, food processor, hand-held electric mixer and a blender are indispensable.

Basic Techniques

I have written the recipes with the following techniques in mind. You may be familiar with some of them, but read on. None of these procedures are complicated or difficult, and good basic techniques lead to creative, elegant, enjoyable meals.

Roasting Peppers

Any kind of pepper can be cooked over a gas flame, over red hot coals or in a very hot oven. The intense heat chars the thin skin, turning it black, and infuses the flesh with a toasty flavor. The charred skin slips right off, leaving soft, silky, delicious peppers.

Gas flame method: Using tongs, hold the pepper over the hottest part of the flame, rotating it until the entire pepper is black. Place the pepper in a plastic bag, seal and let it "steam" for 15 to 20 minutes. Peel when cool.

Oven method: Preheat oven to 450°F, place peppers on a heavy sheet pan and roast in oven until all sides are black, rotating as necessary. Steam in plastic bag for 15 to 20 minutes. Peel when cool.

Grill method: Cook peppers over red hot coals until the skin blackens, rotating as needed. Steam in a plastic bag and peel.

Sometimes I roast a bunch of peppers at one time and store them, peeled, in jars, covered with some olive oil. If you are doing one or two peppers, you might as well do a few more and make good use of your oven heat or live coals. Peppers packed in oil will keep for a few weeks in the refrigerator.

Peeling Fresh Tomatoes

Bring a large pot of water to boil. Remove tomato cores and make an X-shaped incision in the bottom of each tomato. Drop tomatoes into boiling water for 3 to 10 seconds, depending on the ripeness (shorter for ripe tomatoes, longer for underripe). Remove from water and plunge into cold water immediately. Peel with ease.

Blanching

To blanch means to partially cook an item in boiling water (or fat). Always use a large pot to give the vegetables plenty of room to move about freely. Salting the water helps green vegetables retain their bright color and perks up the natural flavor of almost all vegetables.

Bring a large pot of salted water to boil; have ready a large bowl of ice water. Drop the vegetables into the boiling water and cook for 1 to 3 minutes—larger pieces take longer than smaller ones, and root vegetables take longer than most other types. Remove vegetables, and immediately plunge them into the ice water. If you are blanching several kinds of vegetables, cook each kind separately, remove with a slotted spoon or a wire mesh and save the boiling water for the next batch.

Sautéing

To sauté means to cook quickly in a small amount of fat, moving the pan to toss the ingredients. Usually, constant high heat is used, but occasionally a lower temperature is required. Use a large sauté pan with sloped sides—you'll be able to toss the foods in the pan without using any utensils.

While on the subject of sauté, I'd like to clarify what is meant by "coat the pan with oil." Different foods and cooking styles require varying amounts of fat; however, there is a base quantity necessary for almost any sauté. Pour some oil into a pan, swirl the pan, allowing the oil to completely coat the bottom of the pan. Pour the excess out and save it for another time.

Washing Greens

Choose leafy greens that are crisp, unbruised, full and healthy. To clean greens, fill the sink with cold water, submerge the greens, gently move them about, and then remove from the water. Repeat using clean water if there is still a lot of dirt remaining. Dry greens in a lettuce spinner or between two dry, lint-free towels. Store greens in a sealed plastic bag in the vegetable drawer of your refrigerator. If you will be using the greens within the hour, you may store them in a bowl, covered with a damp cloth or paper towel. The idea is to seal the moisture in without creating a wet environment.

Clarifying Butter

Clarified butter is used for high-heat cooking. "Raw," whole, or unclarified butter has a very low burning point, which makes it unsatisfactory when the heat is high.

To clarify, melt butter in a heavy saucepan over moderate heat. When the butter has completely melted, skim the foam from the surface and discard. Carefully pour the butter into a container, leaving the milky liquid behind. Discard the milky liquids and any solids. Clarified butter will keep in the refrigerator for a couple of weeks. Use 1¼ pounds of butter to make about 1 pound of clarified butter.

Making Ghee

Ghee is an eastern Indian ingredient, inspired by the region's intense heat and lack of refrigeration. Properly made ghee will last for months unrefrigerated. Also, ghee has an even higher smoking point than clarified butter, and it imparts a very pleasant nutty flavor to foods cooked in it.

Follow the same procedure for making clarified butter, repeating two more times. Strain through a double thickness of cheesecloth. Two pounds of butter makes about 1 pound of ghee.

Cooking and Cleaning Mushrooms

This book calls for a variety of mushrooms, some delicate and fragile, others meaty and sturdy. Fragile mushrooms include: chanterelle, shiitake, cèpes, oyster and enoki. Like any delicate product, these require special attention during the cooking process to preserve the shape and flavor. The sturdy mushrooms are domestic button, brown domestic, porcini, Italian field, porta bella and morel. The best way to clean *only* the buttons and brown domestics is to submerge them in water, toss them about, remove from the water and then discard the water. Do not pour the water out with the mushrooms because the loosened dirt will slide back onto the mushrooms. The same goes for washing them in the sink; remove the mushrooms from the water, *then* drain the water. All other mushrooms should be wiped clean with a damp cloth. As you pick the pine needles and soil from the chanterelles and carefully brush the "imported" dirt from the Italian field mushrooms, just be thankful you don't have three cases to do!

To cook sturdy mushrooms, sear them in a small amount of fat over very high heat until they turn golden brown. It is nearly impossible to burn mushrooms due to their high water content, so please crank up that heat and go to town. Searing seals in the juices and, at the same time, brings out the natural flavors. If the recipe calls for the addition of a liquid, add it toward the end of cooking. Always use a large pan to cook mushrooms, or cook in batches, because crowding causes excess steam, which produces wimpy, soft, bland mushrooms. The delicate mushrooms must be cooked in a small amount of liquid over moderate heat. This method preserves their shape and helps retain their subtle flavor.

Mushroom soy sauce, made from soy beans and mushrooms, is indispensable in vegetarian cooking, especially when cooking mushrooms. You can add dashes of mushroom soy at the finish to really perk up the flavors. Mushroom soy is quite salty, so do not add any salt during the cooking process.

Cutting Vegetables

Basic common sense dictates the size and shape of most cut vegetables. A batch of any vegetable should be cut cleanly and neatly into pieces of uniform size. The shape does depend on the recipe, but visualize the size of forks, spoons and mouths. It is most important to cut bite-size pieces when making soups, stews and pasta sauces. Dazzle your guests with beautiful jewel-like, perfectly cut vegetables.

Chop—To chop is to cut into irregularly shaped pieces. This method is used when the finished product will not be seen, as in stocks or in the case of soups and sauces where the vegetable is pureed. The size of chop—coarse, fine, medium or rough—depends on the ingredient and use. For example, coarse chop is often used for nuts and it means to chop them into fairly large pieces. Fine and medium chop mean just that, and rough chop is usually used for soups or stocks, where uniformity of size and shape is unimportant. Rough chop for onions can be wedge shape (see "Cutting Onions") because it is the easiest and fastest to do.

Diagonal Cut (See illustration page 22)—Most commonly used with long cylindrical vegetables such as carrots, parsnips, zucchini, squash, cucumbers, Japanese eggplant, and some smaller vegetables like green beans and asparagus. A large diagonal cut across produces nicely oval slices. For very fat or thick vegetables, you can alter the diagonal cut by first slicing lengthwise, then making diagonal cuts across.

Roll Cut (See illustration page 22)—This type of cut is used in many Asian dishes, generally for long cylindrical shaped vegetables, such as carrots, parsnips, Japanese eggplant, squash or zucchini. Trim the stem end, make the first diagonal cut at a 30 degree angle, rotate the vegetable about 30 degrees and cut again. Depending on the length, the shapes are like julienne or large, fat dice with many sides. The shape is good for stews, ragouts, some pasta sauces and showy salads.

Julienne—In traditional continental cooking, julienne is a strip ⅛ by ⅛ by 2½ inches. For recipes in this book, though, cut shapes ¼ by ¼ by 1½ to 2 inches, closer to a classic "batonnet."

Dice (See illustration page 22)—Dice shape is a square or slightly rectangular cube. Small is ¼ inch, medium is ½ inch and large is 1 inch.

Sliver—A sliver is best described as a shape larger than a "shred" but finer than a "batonnet." The easiest way to cut slivers is to cut the vegetable into thin oval shapes (diagonal cut), then cut each oval lengthwise into very thin, long pieces.

Mince—To mince is to chop into very fine particles. Usually herbs are minced.

Cutting Onions

There really are specific ways to cut an onion. And, no, there isn't a special trick to no-tear cutting except to walk away from the enemy. The natural shape of the onion requires the application of certain cutting techniques that differ from other vegetables.

There are three basic shapes used in this book: dice, wedge and slice. *To dice,* trim stem end, cut onion in half and peel. Depending on the size of the dice, make horizontal cuts *through* the inside of the onion, just to the root, then make vertical cuts across the top from stem end to root end. Finish by cutting across the grain. *To cut wedge shapes,* trim root and stem end of the onion and cut

(continued on page 24)

1. Diagonal Cut
   Produces oval slices
   from cylindrical
   shapes.

2. Roll Cut
   After a diagonal cut,
   rotate vegetable 30°
   and cut again. Rotate
   and cut again until
   finished.

3. Dice
   a. Cut curved edges
   of cylindrical or round
   vegetables until you
   have a square or
   rectangular shape.
   b. Cut thin or thick
   slices depending on
   the size dice you
   want.
   c. Stack slices and cut
   again to produce
   strips.
   d. Stack strips and
   cut again to produce
   dice.

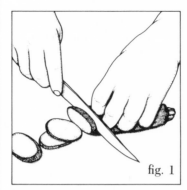

fig. 1

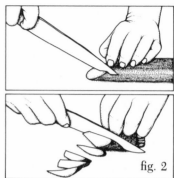

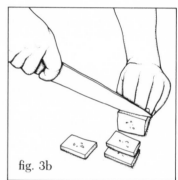

fig. 2

fig. 3a

fig. 3b

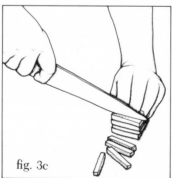

fig. 3c

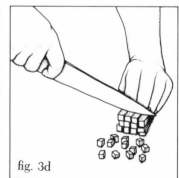

fig. 3d

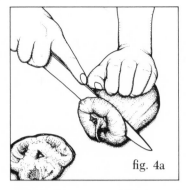

fig. 4a

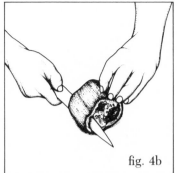

fig. 4b

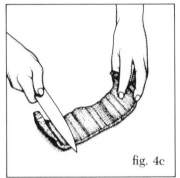

fig. 4c

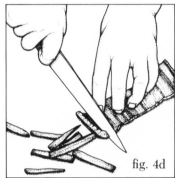

fig. 4d

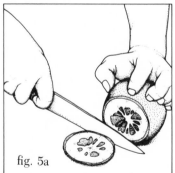

fig. 5a

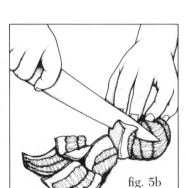

fig. 5b

4. Cutting Peppers

   a. Slice off top (stem) and bottom leaving a cylinder with seeds and ribs attached.

   b. Slice along inner surface to remove ribs and seeds.

   c. Cut through cylinder crosswise and flatten the band of pepper.

   d. Cut into slivers, julienne or wider strips as needed.

5. Peeling Citrus Fruit

   a. Cut top and bottom from the fruit.

   b. Stand fruit on flat (cut) surface and cut from top to bottom, removing the peel and white membrane.

in half. Peel and begin cutting *with* the grain, root to stem. Wedges can be ¼ inch wide to 1 or 1½ inches wide. *To slice,* trim the stem end, cut onion in half and peel. Begin cutting across the grain, creating half-moons shapes.

Toasting Nuts and Seeds

Place nuts or seeds on a sheet pan, bake at 350° F for 5 to 10 minutes, depending on the nut. Bigger, meatier nuts, such as hazelnuts, filberts, walnuts and almonds require more time; smaller, more delicate nuts, such as pine nuts, cashews, pecans and peanuts, require less time. When their fragrance fills the air, check the nuts, remove from the oven when golden brown, and cool. If you are really pressed for time, you can toast nuts in a sauté pan, tossing them in the pan over low heat. This method is not as thorough, nor does it toast the nuts as nicely, but in a pinch it will work. Nuts still warm from the oven are usually soggy; they will crisp as they cool.

Peeling Citrus Fruit

If a recipe calls for sectioned grapefruit or orange pieces, the fruit must first be peeled. Cut off both ends and place cut side down on a cutting board. Using a sharp knife, cut from top to bottom, following the curve of the fruit, removing the peel. Be sure to remove the white membrane as well. (See illustrations 5a, 5b on page 23.)

Caramelizing Onions

To caramelize is to brown the sugars in certain foods using heat. A common myth is that caramelizing is produced by the addition of sugar, sweet wines or vinegars. To caramelize onions, all that is needed is butter or oil and onions. Melt the butter in a heavy skillet, add the onions and brown over high heat until golden, reduce heat and cook until onions are soft, sweet and seductively aromatic. A few recipes in this book call for the addition of wine or vinegar to intensify the taste.

Preparing Herbs

Wash parsley by dunking it in cold water two or three times and gently but thoroughly shaking the water from it. Herbs, including parsley, should be very dry before you begin cutting them. Remove the leaves from the stems and use herb knives or a very sharp French knife to mince. *Do not overwork the herbs*, or you'll just have a dark green soggy mess.

The flavor of fresh herbs is more subtle than dry herbs. Heat destroys their delicate bouquet quickly, so always add them toward the end of cooking or at the very last minute.

If substituting fresh herbs for dry, use three times fresh for the amount of dried called for in the recipe.

Reducing

Reducing or boiling down liquids intensifies the flavor. If you are going to reduce a sauce or stock, add the salt *after* reducing, otherwise you'll have an overly salty final product.

Shaving Corn

To shave corn simply means to cut the kernels off the cob. Use a very sharp or serrated knife. If you cut rather slowly the kernels won't fly all over the kitchen!

Steaming

To steam is to cook by direct contact with steam, as opposed to cooking in water. Electric and stove-top steamers are easy and convenient to use. Or set 3- or 4-inch high wire rack in a large pan, place the food on the rack and fill the pan with 2 inches of water. Do not let the water touch the food. Bring water to a boil, and cook, covered, until food is done. Check the water from time to time and replenish if it has boiled away.

Making a Roux

To make a roux, melt the butter or heat the oil in a heavy-bottomed saucepan. When the fat is hot but not smoking, add the flour, stirring constantly. Reduce the heat to low and stir the sandy mixture until it turns the desired color and consistency. A fully cooked roux, be it a light or blond, medium or dark one, will be sandy and slightly dry. It will come away from the sides of the pan.

For white sauces, make a blond or light roux so that it will not discolor the sauce or soup. The flavor of a light roux is less assertive than a darker one. A medium roux should have a slightly nutty aroma and can be a little darker than the color of a peanut. Dark roux is very nutty and has a deep brown color. The intense flavor and color play an important role in many soups and sauces.

It is fairly easy to burn a roux if the heat is too high or the pot goes unattended for too long. Remember that butter burns easily. But the most common mistake is undercooking a roux, which gives the food an unpleasant raw taste.

Basic Tips

The following tips and suggestions will help you use this book and understand certain phrases.

TIP #1. *Always* read the recipe through once or twice before shopping, prepping or cooking.

TIP #2. Have all your ingredients ready. If a recipe calls for an ingredient to be diced, dice it before you begin the paragraph directions.

TIP #3. Preheat the oven if necessary.

TIP #4. "Taste and adjust seasoning." Many times I have left a finished (or what I thought was finished) pot of food to rest, and upon retasting a while later, I discovered it lacking in something—acid, salt, richness or spiciness. Time, heat and other natural variances change the appearance and taste of foods.

Use your taste buds. Food differs from region to region, month to month and so does your palate, therefore tasting and adjusting are imperative. Remember, you can always add more, but you can't take away.

TIP #5. "Pinch" traditionally means just that, whatever you can get between thumb and forefinger. My pinches, I confess, are more generous. When you see "pinch" in this book, just think about two or three conventional pinches.

TIP #6. "Salt and pepper, to taste." After the initial salt and pepper have been added and the food is almost done, you may need to add additional salt or pepper. Go easy on the salt—it should not be a taste or even a sensation but rather a vehicle for enhancing the natural flavors of food. While meat, poultry, fish and seafood have a relatively high natural salt content, vegetarian cooking does require the addition of some salt.

Like salt, black pepper and other hotter peppers should be added with discretion. Too much pepper will reduce food to a flat, offensive, painful experience, rather than enlivening the dish.

TIP #7. When buying sun-dried tomatoes, try to find "dry" tomatoes sold in bulk. The sun-dried tomatoes sold presoaked in olive oil are at least three times as expensive as those sold dry. To reconstitute, place tomatoes in a bowl, cover with boiling water and let stand 20 minutes to one hour. Drain and use.

Basic Recipes

Basic Mayonnaise

2 large egg yolks
1 Tb. vinegar,
   preferably white wine
   or champagne
1 Tb. Dijon mustard
1 cup vegetable oil
½ cup olive oil
Juice from one lemon
½ tsp. white pepper
Pinch salt and cayenne

Combine yolks, vinegar and mustard in a small bowl. Add half the oil drop by drop, whisking all the while. When an emulsion has formed, add the remaining oil in a thin stream, whisking constantly. Add the lemon juice, pepper, salt and cayenne. Taste and adjust seasoning.

    Makes about 2 cups.

Fresh Tomato Sauce

2 medium onions,
   medium dice
6 cloves garlic, minced
1 tsp. each dry thyme,
   oregano, and basil
½ cup olive oil
3 pounds ripe tomatoes,
   chopped (about 15 to
   17 large tomatoes)
Salt and pepper, to taste

Cook onions, garlic and herbs in olive oil until onions are soft. Add chopped tomatoes and cook over moderate heat until soft, about 10 to 15 minutes. Cool slightly. Puree in batches using a blender. Strain through a fine wire mesh or strainer to remove the seeds and skin. Return to a saucepan and heat. Season with salt and pepper. Reduce to thicken sauce.

    Makes 3 to 4 cups.

COOK'S NOTE:

If a rich sauce is desired, add 3 tablespoons of unsalted butter in small pieces, allowing each piece to melt before adding another.

Canned Tomato Sauce

This sauce has quite a bit more texture than the preceding fresh sauce. Both are good in their own way.

Cook onions, garlic and herbs in olive oil until onions are soft. Add red wine and cook over high heat for 1 minute. Add chopped tomatoes, reduce heat and cook for 10 to 15 minutes. Cool slightly. Puree in batches, using a blender. Return to saucepan and heat. Season with salt, pepper and sugar.
    Makes 3 to 4 cups.

2 medium onions,
    medium dice
8 cloves garlic, minced
2 tsp. each dry oregano,
    thyme and basil
½ cup olive oil
Splash of red wine
2 cans (28 ounces each)
    whole tomatoes,
    seeded and chopped
Salt and pepper, to taste
2 tsp. sugar (see
    COOK'S NOTE)

COOK'S NOTE:

Adding a bit of sugar helps temper the acid of canned tomatoes.

Five-Pepper Mix

Many specialty or natural-food stores carry this delightful spice blend, or you can easily make your own.

Combine all ingredients and grind.

2 Tb. white
    peppercorns
3 Tb. black peppercorns
2 Tb. whole allspice
4 Tb. red peppercorns
4 Tb. green
    peppercorns

Chinese Five-Spice Powder

1½ Tb. Szechuan peppercorns, ground
1 Tb. fennel seed, ground
6 star anise, ground
7 cloves, ground
1 inch cinnamon stick, crushed
1 tsp. coriander, ground

Combine all ingredients and blend well.

Pickling Spice

1 Tb. celery seed
1 Tb. mustard seed
1 Tb. white peppercorns
1 Tb. black peppercorns
1 Tb. whole allspice
10 bay leaves

Combine all ingredients.

Cranberry Relish

3 cups fresh cranberries
1 cup dried apple slices, rough chop
½ cup dried apricots, rough chop
½ cup currants
1 cup orange juice
2 inches cinnamon stick
10 cloves
5 coriander seeds, ground
2 cardamom pods, ground
1 Tb. whole allspice, ground zest from 1 lemon and 1 orange
3 Tb. apple cider vinegar
Salt and pepper, to taste

Place all ingredients in a nonaluminum saucepan. Cook over low heat until the cranberries are soft and slightly broken apart. Taste and adjust for salt and pepper.
    Makes 8 to 10 servings.

Basic Polenta

Polenta is a fabulous, hearty, robust and simple dish to prepare. You will be amazed at how versatile it can be, and a basic polenta dish costs pennies to make. Several recipes in this book call for a variation of this standard recipe. Use coarse cornmeal; some stores sell this cornmeal under the name "polenta."

Place water, butter, garlic, salt and pepper in a large pot. Bring water to a boil. Slowly add cornmeal, whisking constantly. When all the cornmeal has been added, reduce heat to very low and cook, stirring constantly, for 10 to 15 minutes. The polenta should be thick and creamy. Taste and adjust seasoning. If the recipe calls for polenta shapes, pour into pan, spread evenly and smooth the surface. If you will be serving the polenta soft, cover and keep warm until ready to serve. You may thin it with a little water just before serving.

Makes 6 to 8 servings.

6 cups water
4 Tb. unsalted butter
3 cloves garlic, minced
Salt and pepper, to taste
2 cups coarse yellow cornmeal

COOK'S NOTE:

To prevent lumps, whisk constantly as you add the cornmeal, and stir frequently as it cooks.

Small Tastes

Small Tastes are little appetite teasers, smaller than classic appetizers. Generally, these are bite-sized tidbits of food, ready to eat out-of-hand. Most go well with a before-dinner round of cocktails, wine or beer. Or plan a cocktail or dinner party around an assortment of these dishes, followed by a large pot of soup served with plenty of bread and butter. Small Tastes also make great snacks to have around the house for the family and any unexpected guests.

Tri-Pepper Polenta Squares

*T*hese crusty, creamy dense polenta squares are addictive and satisfying. Luckily, they are really easy to make. You can make the polenta in the morning—even better, make it the day before—and fry just before serving. Keep the fried polenta squares warm in a 200° F oven.

Sauté the onion in the butter until soft; set aside. Make the Basic Polenta, adding the grated cheeses just before it is done. Stir well. Add the onion, diced peppers, herbs, salt and pepper to taste. While polenta is still warm, pour into a 9 x 12-inch baking pan and spread evenly to the edges. Brush the surface with a little olive oil. Refrigerate until ready to use or at least 4 to 5 hours.

Cut polenta into 1½-inch squares. Heat some olive oil in a large skillet. When hot, add the squares in batches; do not crowd them. Cook on all sides until golden brown.

Makes about 80 squares.

1 large red onion, small dice
3 Tb. unsalted butter
Basic Polenta (see page 31)
⅓ pound natural smoked cheese, such as Bruderbasil, grated
¼ pound sharp cheddar cheese, grated
1 red pepper, small dice
2 small green peppers, small dice
1 small yellow pepper, small dice
4 to 6 red jalapeno peppers, minced
Pinch dry thyme and oregano
Salt and pepper, to taste
Olive oil, for frying

COOK'S NOTE:

Make sure the polenta squares are golden brown before flipping. If you turn them too soon, they will stick to the pan.

Onion Cakes
with Spicy Plum Sauce

*S*avory *little pancakes with a hint of hot pepper, these onion cakes are simple and fast to make. They provide an interesting snack with a subtle Asian flavor.*

2 medium onions, sliced very thin

¼ cup sesame oil

1 cup all-purpose flour

4 large eggs, lightly beaten

1 cup Vegetable Stock (see page 69)

¼ cup soy sauce

3 Tb. rice wine vinegar

3 cloves garlic, minced

8 scallions, minced

1 tsp. red pepper flakes

1 tsp. black pepper

Salt, to taste

Peanut oil

Spicy Plum Sauce (recipe follows)

Cilantro sprigs, for garnish

Sauté onions in sesame oil until soft; set aside without draining the oil. Combine flour, eggs and vegetable stock to form a paste. Add all the remaining ingredients, except the peanut oil and the plum sauce. Stir well. Add the sautéed onion and the excess sesame oil. Allow batter to rest for 20 to 30 minutes.

Heat some peanut oil in a 5- or 6-inch nonstick skillet. Spoon 2 to 3 tablespoons of batter into pan, swirling the batter around as if you were making crepes or a thin omelet. When the edges start to brown, flip the cake and cook on the other side. Finish the remaining batter in this way. Thin the batter with a little water if necessary. Keep the cakes warm in the oven while making the rest.

To serve, fold each pancake in quarters, and arrange on a large platter. Garnish with sprigs of cilantro, and pass the Spicy Plum Sauce.

Makes 6 to 8 servings.

SPICY PLUM SAUCE

Combine all ingredients in a nonreactive saucepan. Bring to a boil, reduce heat and simmer for 1 hour. Add a little water if mixture gets too thick. Puree in a blender or food processor until smooth. Taste and adjust seasoning.

Makes about 2½ cups.

1 cup plums, pitted, or
  1 cup plum preserves
½ cup roasted red
  pepper, medium dice
¼ cup apricots, pitted
  and chopped
1 handful raisins
6 dates, pitted and
  chopped
4 cloves garlic, minced
1 Tb. black vinegar
3 Tb. red wine vinegar
¼ cup balsamic vinegar
1 Tb. soy sauce
2 tsp. red pepper flakes
1 tsp. black pepper

Spanish Tortilla
with Romesco Sauce

This is the Spanish version of the Italian frittata, or a fancy omelet with potatoes. The simplicity of the frittata is refreshing and the zesty sauce that accompanies it is a perfect companion. This dish makes a charming brunch offering for those who feel morning doesn't begin without eggs in one form or another. A cold tortilla makes a wonderful midnight snack.

2 large yellow onions, medium wedge cut

½ cup olive oil

5 medium baking potatoes, cut ¼-inch thick half moons

6 cloves garlic, sliced thin

2 tsp. dry thyme

Salt and pepper

10 large eggs, lightly beaten

Romesco Sauce (recipe follows)

Preheat oven to 350°F.

Cook the onions in the olive oil in a 12-inch or larger nonstick, ovenproof skillet until soft. Add the potatoes, garlic, thyme, salt and pepper; cook over low heat, stirring often, until the potatoes are tender but not too soft. Slowly pour the eggs into the pan, stir and cook for 3 to 4 minutes or until eggs begin to set. Place pan in preheated oven and bake for 20 to 30 minutes, until eggs are compeletly set. Let tortilla sit for 20 minutes before removing from the pan. Invert onto a large plate. Cut into wedge shapes and serve at room temperature.

Makes 6 to 8 servings.

ROMESCO SAUCE

2 medium roasted red peppers, peeled and seeded

½ cup tomatoes, peeled and seeded

3 cloves garlic

⅓ cup sun-dried tomatoes

½ cup blanched almonds, chopped

¼ cup balsamic vinegar

Splash of sherry vinegar

1 tsp. red pepper flakes

⅔ to 1 cup olive oil

Salt and pepper, to taste

Puree all ingredients except olive oil, salt and pepper in a blender. With the machine running, add the olive oil in a thin stream. An emulsion will form. Remove from the blender, add the salt and pepper. Taste and adjust seasoning. Serve at room temperature.

Makes about 2 cups.

COOK'S NOTE:

If you like spicy food, add more red pepper flakes or a dash of Tabasco sauce.

Five-Spice Tea Cooked Eggs

*T*hese eggs look like porcelain treasures—the lustrous white egg is a canvas for a delicate, amber-colored lace design. Their unique taste and dramatic presentation make them a popular item for parties. I like to bring these along when I'm invited to dinner at a friend's house as they travel well and are quite impressive.

Place the eggs in a small saucepan, cover with water and bring to a boil. Reduce heat and simmer for 5 to 8 minutes. Remove eggs from pan and cool. When eggs are cool, gently rap on a hard surface to crack the shell. You must keep the membrane *intact* because the eggs will be cooked again. Cracking the shells in this manner allows the color and flavor of the liquid to penetrate through to the egg. Combine all the remaining ingredients and add to the water. Gently submerge the eggs, bring to a boil and immediately reduce the heat. Simmer, covered, for 1 hour. Remove from the heat and let sit in the liquid for 4 to 6 hours. To serve, peel eggs and cut in halves or quarters. Store *unpeeled* eggs in the seasoned liquid.

Makes 6 to 8 servings.

8 fresh eggs, room temperature
½ cup black tea leaves
1 cup soy sauce
Splash of mirin or sweet sherry (see **COOK'S NOTE**)
10 star anise
2 Tb. fennel seed, bruised (see **COOK'S NOTE**)
12 whole cloves, bruised
2 Tb. anise seed, bruised
2 Tb. coriander, bruised
2 2-inch sticks cinnamon
2 tsp. red pepper flakes
3 cloves garlic, minced

COOK'S NOTE:

Make the eggs a day ahead so that the flavor can fully develop. These eggs can be stored in the refrigerator for 3 to 4 days.

To bruise the spices use a mortar and pestle or just partially grind them using a spice grinder. If you don't own either tool, simply smash them with a blunt object on a hard surface!

Mirin is a Japanese sweet rice wine used primarily in cooking. It can be found in most Asian supermarkets. Sweet sherry can be used as a substitute.

Stuffed Pasta Wheels

U*sually I prefer fresh pasta to dry, but sometimes dry pasta works just as well or better. Dry lasagne noodles with ruffled edges work perfectly for this dish.*

1 pound spinach lasagne
noodles

Olive oil

1½ pounds fresh ricotta
cheese

2 cloves garlic, minced

¼ pound Asiago cheese,
grated fine

¼ pound fontina cheese,
grated fine

½ cup sun-dried
tomatoes, chopped
fine

½ cup walnuts, chopped
fine

¾ cup minced fresh
herbs (see page 12)

1 tsp. red pepper flakes

1 tsp. white pepper

Salt, to taste

Flat leaf parsley, for
garnish

Cook the noodles until just tender in a large roasting pan, heavy baking pan or large pot filled with salted boiling water (see COOK'S NOTE). Remove from the water and drain. Lightly brush both sides of each noodle with oil and cover with a damp towel until ready to use.

Combine the remaining ingredients. Taste and adjust seasoning.

Lay a noodle out on a cutting board or flat surface. Wipe any excess oil from surface. Spread some of the ricotta mixture the length of the noodle and roll up, keeping the filling inside the pinwheel. Repeat with the remaining noodles and cheese mixture. When you have finished, cut each pinwheel in half, so that each piece has a ruffled side. Arrange on a large platter, ruffled side up, and garnish with flat leaf parsley. Serve at room temperature.

Makes about 30 pinwheels.

COOK'S NOTE:

The pasta must be cooked gently in slowly boiling water so that the ribbons do not break or tear. The ideal pot is a long and heavy one that can be placed on a burner and also accommodate the full length of the pasta. That way the ribbons will retain their shape.

Roast Pepper Wrapped Hearts of Palm

I have yet to find fresh hearts of palm in this country, but canned ones work well in this recipe. Marinating the hearts helps to remove any tin taste that might have developed.

Combine the marinade ingredients and pour over the hearts of palm. Marinate for 4 to 6 hours.

Carefully peel and seed the peppers, cut into strips about 3 inches wide, set aside.

Combine the remaining ingredients. Drain the hearts of palm, reserving the marinade for another use. Carefully spread some of the cheese filling on each pepper strip, almost covering the strip. Lay a half piece of palm on top of the cheese, roll the pepper around the palm. A small portion of the palm should extend out of each roll. Roll all the hearts of palm in this fashion. Serve at room temperature.

Makes about 20 pieces.

MARINADE
1 cup olive oil
3 cloves garlic
2 Tb. coarse-grain mustard
½ cup sherry vinegar
1 tsp. black pepper
Pinch salt

2 cans (13 ounces each) hearts of palm, each piece sliced in half, lengthwise
2 medium red peppers, roasted
2 medium yellow peppers, roasted
2 medium green peppers, roasted
1 pound cream cheese, preferably without stabilizers or gums
½ pound Gruyère cheese, grated fine
¾ cup mixed fresh herbs, minced
(see page 12)
1 tsp. red pepper flakes
Salt and pepper, to taste

Chili Roasted Mixed Nuts

*O**kay, nuts are addicting in themselves... and the last thing we need is to increase the temptation. Go for it. These make a fun food gift to bring along to parties, dinners or outdoor events. The complex spice combination and the hot pepper make these nuts impossible to ignore!*

2 Tb. dried hot red peppers
2 Tb. cumin seed
2 Tb. whole coriander
1½ Tb. dry oregano
1 Tb. black pepper
1 Tb. garlic salt
1 Tb. red peppercorns
1 Tb. paprika
1 tsp. turmeric
1 tsp. whole allspice
¼ pound unsalted butter
2 pounds assorted nuts

Preheat oven to 400° F.

Grind all the spices in a grinder. Melt the butter, add the spices and stir well. Place the nuts in a large bowl, pour the spice butter over the nuts and mix well. Divide the nuts between two sheet pans and bake for 15 to 20 minutes. Remove from oven and let cool. Serve at room temperature.

COOK'S NOTE:

The nuts will be soft and soggy when you first remove them from the oven. Don't worry; they will crisp as they cool.

Pear and Cherry Tomatoes
with Herbed Goat Cheese

These bite-sized jewels are savory and juicy. They explode in your mouth, releasing a unique burst of flavor. Perfect for hot summer days, they require no time at the oven or stove. A wonderful way to use plentiful summer tomatoes.

Combine all the ingredients except the tomatoes. Mix well and adjust sesaoning. Cut each tomato in half and pat cut surface dry. Spoon a small amount of cheese onto cut tomato, top with opposite color tomato. Make all the tomatoes in this fashion. Garnish with sprigs of flat leaf parsley. Serve at room temperature.

    Makes 6 to 8 servings.

½ pound pine nuts, chopped fine

½ pound cream cheese, softened

½ pound mild goat cheese, such as Bucheron or Montrachet

2 cloves garlic, minced

½ cup mixed fresh herbs, minced (see page 12)

1 tsp. white pepper

½ tsp. cardamom pods, ground

Pinch of nutmeg

Salt, to taste

1 pint cherry tomatoes

1 pint yellow pear tomatoes

Flat leaf parsley, for garnish

Spinach Mushroom Filo Triangles

*F*ilo is the paper-thin dough used in many Middle Eastern dishes, including baklava. Many large supermarket chains carry filo in the frozen-food department. These spinach mushroom pastries are rich, buttery and satisfying. Once you've made the filling, the rest goes really fast. The triangles can be prepared a couple days ahead, refrigerated and baked just before serving.

1 large onion, small dice
3 cloves garlic, minced
1 Tb. prepared chili powder
1 Tb. dry thyme
⅓ cup olive oil
¾ pound mushrooms, coarse chop
2 bunches spinach, cleaned and cut into 1-inch pieces
½ pound ricotta cheese
¾ pound feta cheese
¾ cup walnuts, chopped fine
1 tsp. coriander, ground
½ tsp. cayenne
½ tsp. nutmeg
Salt and pepper, to taste

Cook onion, garlic, chili powder and thyme in some olive oil over low heat until onion is soft. Place in a large bowl and set aside. In the same pan, cook the mushrooms in some olive oil over high heat until golden brown. Add to the onions. Once again in the same pan, cook the spinach until it wilts. When cool, squeeze the excess liquid from the spinach. Add to the onions and mushrooms. Set aside.

Combine the ricotta, feta, walnuts and spices. Taste and adjust seasoning. When the vegetable mixture is completely cool, combine it with the cheese mixture. Taste and adjust seasoning.

Preheat the oven to 350° F.

To assemble: Lay one sheet of filo out on a large flat surface, brush lightly with some melted butter, sprinkle with about 2 tablespoons of ground almonds, cover with a second sheet of filo, and brush lightly with melted butter. Cut this into thirds lengthwise. Place a rounded tablespoon of filling on the bottom corner of one of the pieces, fold over once, to make a triangle shape, and continue rolling in this fashion, as if you were folding a flag. Roll the other two pieces into triangles. Brush the tops with melted butter and set aside. Continue making triangles three at a time so that the filo dough does not dry out. Bake in the preheated oven for 10 to 12 minutes or until golden brown. Serve piping hot.

Makes about 40 triangles.

1 pound filo dough, thawed (see COOK'S NOTE)

½ pound unsalted butter, melted

2 cups almonds, ground fine

COOK'S NOTE:

Thaw filo dough in the refrigerator overnight or at room temperature for 2 to 4 hours. When working with filo dough, keep it covered with a damp towel at all times to prevent it from drying out.

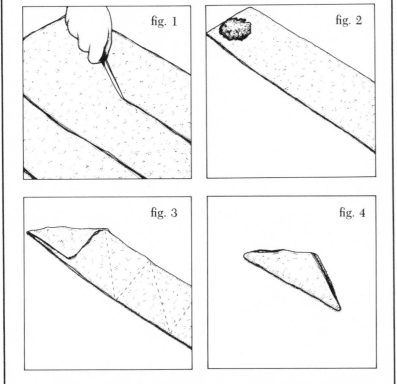

fig. 1

fig. 2

fig. 3

fig. 4

Filo Triangles
1. Cut filo sheets into thirds lengthwise.
2. Place filling on the bottom corner of the strip.
3. Fold over once to make triangle shape and continue rolling as if folding a flag.
4. The final triangle package.

Curried Samosas
with Fire Dipping Sauce

These are tasty little packages filled with savory curried vegetables and potatoes. Traditionally they are deep-fried, but baking works just as well, and frankly, I prefer it. Don't be put off by the long list of ingredients—the list is mostly spices—or the seemingly complex preparation. This dough is simple to make and foolproof. Be prepared to make a second batch after your guests have one taste; these go very quickly. The samosas can also be frozen and then baked on a moment's notice.

DOUGH

1¾ cups all-purpose flour

¼ cup rye flour

1 tsp. salt

4 Tb. unsalted butter, chilled

4 Tb. fruity olive oil

7 to 9 Tb. cold water

Combine the flours and salt. Add the butter in small pieces, using your fingers to mix. When the butter has been incorporated, add the olive oil, mixing with your fingers. Add the cold water one tablespoon at a time until the dough forms a ball and comes away from the sides of the bowl. Knead the dough for 1 or 2 minutes. Cover with a damp towel and set aside. Make the second batch of dough (see COOK'S NOTE), keeping the balls separate, so that it will be easier to measure out.

COOK'S NOTE:

The ingredients listed here will make one batch of dough. Two batches are needed for this recipe, but the dough is easier to handle and measure batch by batch.

1. Place filling on dough round.
2. Fold round in half.

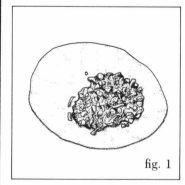

fig. 1

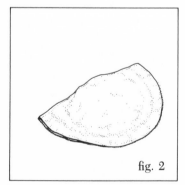

fig. 2

Cook the diced potatoes in salted boiling water until tender but not mushy. Drain and cool.

Cook the onions, garlic, jalapenos, and all the spices in the olive oil over low heat. When the onions are soft, add the tomatoes and cook over high heat for 3 to 4 minutes, stirring constantly. Reduce heat and add the diced green peppers. Cook until the green peppers are tender but not mushy. Add the cilantro and the cooled potatoes, taste and adjust seasoning. The potatoes call for quite a bit of salt; don't be afraid to use *some*.

Preheat oven to 350° F.

To assemble (see illustration on page 44): Divide one dough ball in half and form into a new ball. Cut each new ball into 12 equal pieces, roll into little balls. Using a rolling pin, roll out into little rounds, approximately 4 inches in diameter. Place a tablespoon of filling on one half of the round. With your finger, rub a little water on the edge of the dough, fold one side over and seal using the tines of a fork. (The water helps to seal the pastry). Brush with a little egg and place on a sheet pan. Continue in the same fashion until all the filling has been used. Bake in the preheated oven for 15 to 20 minutes or until golden brown. Serve hot with Fire Dipping Sauce. (Recipe follows)

Makes 8 to 10 servings.

FIRE DIPPING SAUCE

Soak dry chiles in water to cover for 2 to 4 hours. When soft, remove seeds and stem. Puree all the ingredients in a blender until smooth. Taste and adjust seasoning.

Makes about 1 cup.

COOK'S NOTE:

This sauce is pretty hot, but smooth at the same time. Better warn your guests and family members before they taste it!

FILLING

5 medium boiling potatoes, small dice

2 large yellow onions, small dice

8 cloves garlic, minced

3 jalapeno peppers, minced

2 Tb. coriander, ground

1 Tb. cumin seed, ground

1½ tsp. fennel seed, ground

2 tsp. turmeric

1 tsp. caraway seed, ground

3 cardamom pods, ground

1 tsp. black pepper

½ to ¾ cup fruity olive oil

5 large tomatoes, chopped

2 green peppers, small dice

1 cup cilantro, rough chop

Salt, to taste

1 egg, lightly beaten

4 dried ancho or poblano chiles

6 dried small red chiles

2 tomatoes, peeled and seeded

3 cloves garlic

¼ cup sugar

⅛ cup seasoned rice wine vinegar

Splash of red wine vinegar

1 tsp. black pepper

Salt, to taste

Imperial Rolls

These crispy rolls are made with Vietnamese rice paper—huge, round, translucent and very brittle. If you cannot find these exotic rice paper sheets, you can use filo dough instead (see COOK'S NOTE). I must say, the first time I used these rice papers I almost gave up after only three minutes. Be patient and practice a bit. Once you get the hang of it, the rest will go smoothly. Be sure to use plenty of water when spraying the sheets, roll as quickly as possible and keep the sheets covered as you work. A challenge indeed, but well worth the effort. Rice papers, as well as cellophane noodles can be found at any Asian supermarket.

½ pound cellophane noodles

2 large onions, sliced very thin

2 green peppers, sliced thin

6 cloves garlic, minced

2 jalapeno peppers, minced

½ to ⅔ cup sesame oil

7 or 8 medium shiitake mushrooms, sliced very thin

3 carrots, shredded

1 cup mint leaves, chopped

1 bunch basil, chopped

1 bunch cilantro, chopped

5-inch piece ginger, peeled and minced

¾ cup roasted peanuts, chopped

½ cup soy sauce

3 Tb. teriyaki sauce

3 Tb. black rice vinegar

1 Tb. sugar

Juice from one lime

Black pepper, to taste

Soak the cellophane noodles in warm water for 2 to 3 minutes. Cut into 4-inch lengths and drain. Cook in boiling water until done, about 4 to 5 minutes. Drain and set aside.

Cook onions, green peppers, garlic and jalapeno peppers in the sesame oil over high heat until wilted. Stir frequently to prevent burning. When the vegetables are wilted, add the shiitake mushrooms and cook over low heat until they are soft but not mushy. Place in a large bowl and cool. When the mixture is cool, add all the remaining ingredients except the rice paper and vegetable oil. Taste and adjust seasoning.

To assemble (see illustration below): Take one sheet of rice paper out of the package, dip in a large bowl of water, or spray using a plastic spray bottle, and lay out on a flat surface. Quickly place about 3 tablespoons of filling on the bottom of the round and roll up, tucking the ends in as you go. Seal with more water and set aside, seam side down. Make all the rolls in this fashion. Heat about 2 inches of vegetable oil in a large skillet. When the oil is hot, but not smoking, add the rolls in batches and cook until golden brown on all sides. Remove from pan and drain on lint-free towels; do not use paper towels as the wrappers will stick to the paper. Serve immediately.

Makes 6 to 8 servings.

1 package rice paper
  rounds
Vegetable oil, for frying

COOK'S NOTE:

If using filo dough, cut sheets into long rectangles, approximately 6 by 8 inches long. Place some filling at the bottom of each piece of filo dough and roll up, tucking in the ends as you go. Brush with melted unsalted butter to seal. Cook in vegetable oil until golden brown. Be sure to cover the stack of filo dough at all times with a damp cloth to prevent it from drying out.

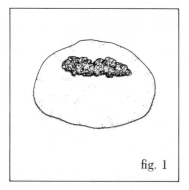

fig. 1

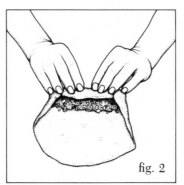

fig. 2

1. Place filling on the bottom of rice paper.
2. Roll up, tucking in the ends as you go.

Mushroom Risotto Croquettes

A rich mushroom risotto is the base for these delicious crispy bites of heaven. The only trick is to resist eating most of the risotto before it is made into the croquettes.

1 large onion, small dice
4 cloves garlic, minced
¼ pound unsalted butter
1½ cups Arborio rice
1 tsp. each dry thyme, basil, oregano
5 to 6 cups strong Mushroom Stock (see page 70)
⅓ pound Asiago cheese, grated fine

1 large onion, small dice
¼ cup olive oil
1 pound mushrooms, fine chop
3 cloves garlic, minced
¼ cup mushroom soy sauce
Splash of dry sherry
½ pound Italian Fontina cheese, cut into ¼-inch cubes
2 large eggs, lightly beaten
1½ cups fine bread crumbs
Vegetable oil, for frying

To make the risotto, cook the onion and garlic in the butter until soft. Add the rice and herbs and cook over moderately high heat for 2 minutes. Add 2 cups of stock, stir well and reduce heat. Cook until the liquid is absorbed, then add 2 more cups of stock. Repeat with remaining stock, stirring frequently. When risotto is soft and creamy, add the grated Asiago cheese. Remove from the heat and set aside. When cool, taste and adjust seasoning.

Cook second onion in some olive oil until soft. Add the mushrooms and garlic and cook over high heat until mushrooms are golden brown and have lost all their liquid. Stir frequently to prevent sticking or burning. Add the mushroom soy and sherry, reduce heat and cook for 1 or 2 more minutes. Taste and adjust seasoning. Add the onion-mushroom mixture to the risotto; mix well.

To form the croquettes, put a cube of Fontina cheese in the palm of your hand, place about 1 rounded tablespoon of risotto around the cheese, completely enclosing the cube. Continue to make risotto "balls" in this fashion. Refrigerate the balls for about 1 hour.

Roll each ball in the eggs, then coat with the bread crumbs. Refrigerate the breaded balls as you go. When all the balls have been breaded, heat the vegetable oil. When the oil is hot, but not smoking, lower a few balls into the pan. *Do not crowd*, or the croquettes will not cook properly! Cook until golden brown and drain on paper towels. Finish cooking in batches. Keep warm in a low oven. Serve hot.

Makes 60 to 70 croquettes.

Salads

Most of these salads are complex and filling enough to be served alone or with some bread or soup. Others could be perfect as the prelude to a full meal. Some of the salads are inspired by the ingredients and flavors of Asia, Italy and Latin America. Try a multiethnic meal or let the salad set the tone for a geographic theme meal.

The dressings in this book are fairly versatile. Many can be used for marinades or dips for vegetables and fruit.

Feel free to experiment with the Basic Mayonnaise recipe as well as the vinaigrettes. These are basic recipes—there are no hard-and-fast rules. Play with the ingredients until you feel comfortable and can create a taste that suits your palate.

Dressings and Vinaigrettes

Walnut or Hazelnut Vinaigrette

A *full-bodied vinaigrette, versatile, rich and full of flavor. This dressing will bring most any salad to life.*

1 clove garlic, minced
2 shallots, sliced paper thin
Pinch salt and pepper
¾ cup walnut or hazelnut oil
¼ cup olive oil
¼ cup (scant) balsamic vinegar
Splash sherry vinegar

Combine garlic, shallots, salt, pepper and some of the oil in a small bowl. Add the remaining oil, whisking constantly. Add balsamic vinegar in a thin stream, whisking constantly. Finish with a splash of sherry vinegar.

Makes about 1¼ cups.

COOK'S NOTE:

The dressing will be temporarily emulsified just after it is made. If it separates, slowly pour it into another bowl, whisking all the while.

Balsamic Vinaigrette

*T*his is one of my favorite vinaigrettes, round and full. Use this for any green salad, vegetable salad or as a marinade. Add more sherry vinegar for a vinaigrette with more bite, or less for a smoother taste.

Combine garlic, shallots and olive oil. Slowly whisk in balsamic vinegar, so that the dressing forms an emulsion. Finish with a splash of sherry vinegar, curry powder, and salt and pepper.
   Makes about 1¼ cups.

1 clove garlic, minced
2 shallots, sliced paper
   thin
1 cup olive oil
¼ cup balsamic vinegar
Splash sherry vinegar
½ tsp. prepared curry
   powder
Salt and pepper, to taste

Four-Vinegar Vinaigrette

*S*herry vinegar has a bright, somewhat intense flavor. Tempererd with other vinegars and oil, it produces a wonderful snappy vinaigrette.

Mix together garlic and olive oil. Whisk in the vinegars one at a time. Add salt and pepper, taste and adjust seasoning.
   Makes about 1¼ cups.

1 clove garlic, minced
1 cup olive oil
3 Tb. sherry vinegar
1 Tb. balsamic vinegar
1 Tb. red wine vinegar
Splash of champagne
   vinegar
Salt and pepper, to taste

Lemon-Mustard Dressing

A full-flavored dressing, good for assertive vegetables, bitter green salads and as a "dip" for just about anything. Serve this drizzled on fresh brown bread, with strong cheeses and red onions for a mouth-watering snack or sandwich.

3 Tb. Dijon Mustard
1 Tb. coarse-grain
    mustard
1 Tb. sweet mustard
2 cloves garlic, minced
Zest from 2 lemons
1 cup olive oil
Juice from 2 lemons
1 Tb. sherry vinegar
1 Tb. apple cider
    vinegar

Mix the mustards, garlic and zest. Slowly add the oil in a thin stream, whisking all the while. When an emulsion forms and all the oil has been added, whisk in the lemon juice and vinegars. Season with salt and pepper.

Makes about 1⅓ cups.

Four-Citrus Vinaigrette

Light, refreshing and lively, this vinaigrette sparkles with flavor. Use the vinaigrette with green salads, with cold vegetables or as a marinade. This would be delicious drizzled over ripe avocados and jicama.

Zest and juice from 1
    orange, 1 lime, 1
    lemon, and 2
    tangerines
1 clove garlic, minced
¾ cup olive oil
¼ cup avocado oil
    (substitute olive oil if
    unavailable)
3 Tb. champagne
    vinegar
Splash sherry vinegar
Salt and pepper, to taste

Combine zest, juices, and garlic. Whisk olive and avocado oils into juices in a thin stream. When an emulsion forms and all the oil has been added, whisk in the vinegars, season with salt and pepper. Taste and adjust seasoning. If you like your vinaigrette to have a real bite, add more sherry vinegar.

Makes about 1½ cups.

Sweet and Sour Dressing

*T*his ranks as one of my favorite dressings. It is thick and creamy without being too heavy. The vinegars and spices add an unusual dimension and make this a versatile dressing that can go with many foods.

Whisk honey, garlic, mayonnaise and spices together. Add the oil in a thin stream, whisking all the while. Slowly whisk in the vinegars. Add salt and pepper, taste and adjust seasoning.

    Makes about 1⅓ cups.

3 Tb. honey
1 clove garlic, minced
4 Tb. mayonnaise
1 tsp. prepared curry powder
1 tsp. coriander, ground
Pinch cayenne
¾ cup olive oil
2 Tb. sherry vinegar
2 Tb. balsamic vinegar
Salt and pepper, to taste

Mayonnaise-Based Dressings

*Y*ou can add almost anything to Basic Mayonnaise (page 28), creating new and unusual tastes appropriate for ethnic or traditional dishes. Here are some ideas:

    Pureed roasted pepper
    Chopped calamata olives Capers
    Green peppercorns
    Coarse-grain mustard
    Pureed roasted garlic
    Wasabi (Japanese horseradish) or prepared horseradish
    Mixed herbs
    Lime, lemon, orange, tangerine or grapefruit zest
    Jalapeno pepper, minced
    Chipotle pepper, pureed
    Ancho pepper, pureed
    Caramelized onion
    Ground spices
    For an Asian flavor, substitute ¼ cup sesame oil for olive or vegetable oil.

Composed Vegetable and Leafy Green Salads

6 small or 2 medium
   yellow beets
6 small Chiogga beets
6 small red beets
Salt and pepper, to taste
Walnut Vinaigrette (see
   page 50)
1 medium yellow onion,
   sliced thin
2 medium heads fennel,
   sliced thin
2 medium firm pears,
   medium dice
1 tart green apple,
   medium dice
2 or 3 bunches
   watercress,
   depending on the size
1 generous cup walnuts,
   toasted

COOK'S NOTE:

You can bake the yellow and pink beets together in the same pan, but bake the red beets separately because they will stain the lighter ones. Chiogga beets are fuchsia or rose-colored beets most commonly found in specialty produce shops or natural food stores.

If the onion is very strong, slice, soak in hot water for 30 minutes, and drain.

Three-Beet Salad
with Pear and Fennel

*R*ed, fuchsia and golden beets sparkle atop fresh fennel, crisp white apple and velvety pears, all dressed with a luscious walnut vinaigrette. One of my favorite fall salads.

Preheat oven to 350° F.

   Remove greens from beets and discard or save for another use. Keeping the red beets separate from pink and yellow, place beets in a shallow dish with a little water, salt and pepper. Bake, covered for 40 minutes to 1 hour until tender but not too soft. Remove from oven and cool in the water. Peel and slice into small wedges; set aside. Dress the yellow and pink beets together and dress the red beets separately with some of the vinaigrette. Dress the onion and fennel, pears and apple with the remaining vinaigrette.

   Place some of the fruit, onion and fennel mixture on top of a small bed of watercress. Arrange the pink and yellow beets on top and place the red beets on last. Garnish with the toasted walnuts.

   Makes 6 to 8 servings.

Warm Potato and Vegetable Salad

A *warm salad of many vegetables and tender cubes of potato makes for a satisfying lunch offering. For a "bigger" taste use the Lemon Mustard Dressing (page 52) instead of the Four-Citrus Vinaigrette.*

Cook the potatoes in salted boiling water until tender but not mushy, drain and cool. Blanch the asparagus and carrots separately.

To make the salad, have all the vegetables ready and the dressing in a large bowl. Bring a large pot of salted water to boil, drop all the vegetables in the water for 1 minute. Do not cook the vegetables, just heat them. After 1 minute remove from water, drain and immediately drop in bowl with the dressing. Toss well and season to taste with salt and pepper. Arrange on a bed of greens.

Makes 6 to 8 servings.

4 red potatoes, medium dice

1 bunch asparagus, 1-inch diagonal cut

1 large carrot, julienne

⅓ pound snow peas, strings removed

1 large yellow pepper, julienne

1 large red pepper, julienne

2 ears corn, shaved

2 tomatoes, medium dice or a handful of Sweet 100's (see COOK'S NOTE)

½ pint yellow pear tomatoes, or 2 yellow tomatoes, small dice

Watercress, frisee, curly endive or any full-flavored leafy green

Four-Citrus Vinaigrette (page 52)

COOK'S NOTE:

Sweet 100's are a very sweet and very small tomato variety.

Tomato, Date and Fennel Salad

This salad is elegant and complex in flavor. The sweet, slightly sour and toasty flavors will delight sophisticated palates. Because it's simple to prepare and serve, it's a good salad to make when the rest of the meal involves a lot of preparation.

¾ cup dates, pitted and chopped

¾ cup black Mission figs, chopped

Juice from 2 oranges

Juice from 1 lemon

Splash of orange or mandarin liqueur

1 large head fennel, sliced thin

1 medium red or yellow onion, sliced thin

4 ripe tomatoes, diced

2 medium heads butter lettuce

1 cup walnuts, toasted

Splash of raspberry vinegar

Walnut Vinaigrette (see page 50)

Combine dates, figs, citrus juices and liqueur in a small bowl; macerate for 2 to 3 hours.

Arrange sliced fennel, onions and diced tomatoes on the lettuce, spoon figs and dates on top and garnish with toasted walnuts. Splash the salad with the raspberry vinegar. Pass the vinaigrette separately or dress the salad just before serving.

Makes 6 to 8 servings.

Warm Red Cabbage Salad

Red cabbage salad can be made with many different ingredients, using the same basic technique. Once you've sautéed the red cabbage, onions, and garlic in a fruity olive oil, finish with vinegar and experiment freely with additional ingredients.

Coat the bottom of a 12-inch sauté pan with the olive oil, and place over moderate heat. When hot, add the garlic and onions and cook for 1 minute. Increase heat and add the red cabbage, stirring constantly. Sauté for about 1 minute more, until the cabbage begins to wilt slightly. Add a splash of the balsamic and apple cider vinegar. Toss and add the salt and pepper. Taste and adjust the seasoning. Serve immediately.

Makes 6 to 8 servings.

Fruity olive oil
3 cloves garlic, minced
2 red onions, sliced thin
1 large head red cabbage, sliced very thin
Balsamic vinegar, splash
Apple cider vinegar, splash
Salt and pepper, to taste

COOK'S NOTE:

Use a large sauté pan or skillet to prepare this dish, or make the cabbage in two batches if necessary. If you try to crowd the ingredients into a small pan, the food will steam and you'll have mushy, wet cabbage and limp onions. Once the oil is hot the rest of the cooking goes very quickly, so be sure to have all the ingredients ready before you begin.

Latin Black Bean and Cabbage

1 cup dry black beans
½ cup olive oil
¼ cup rice wine vinegar
Splash sherry vinegar
1 clove garlic, minced
½ Tb. cumin seed,
  ground
2 tsp. coriander, ground
½ cup cilantro, chopped
Salt and pepper, to taste
Warm Red Cabbage
  Salad ingredients (see
  page 57)
1 green pepper, sliced
  thin
1 orange, sectioned (see
  page 24)
1 small jicama, julienne
  or 1 large apple,
  sliced thin, if jicama
  is unavailable
½ cup pumpkin seeds,
  toasted

Soak black beans in 5 cups of water overnight.

Cook the black beans in their soaking water for 45 minutes to one hour, or until tender but not mushy. Drain and cool. Marinate the cooled beans in the olive oil, vinegars, garlic, cumin, coriander, and half the cilantro. Season with salt and pepper.

Make the basic Warm Red Cabbage Salad, sautéing the green peppers with the cabbage. Place a portion on each plate. Arrange some of the orange sections and jicama on top of the cabbage, follow with 2 tablespoons of the beans per serving. Top with toasted pumpkin seeds and garnish with the remaining cilantro.

Makes 6 to 8 servings.

COOK'S NOTE:

Remember the cabbage portion of this dish should be warm, so work fast while assembling.

California Cabbage

Add the apple, fennel and onion to the cabbage. Cook according to the directions for Warm Red Cabbage Salad, adding the oil-cured olives and the feta cheese just before it's done. Mix well. Garnish with the pistachio nuts.

Makes 6 to 8 servings.

3 tart green apples, sliced thin

1 head fennel, sliced thin

1 red onion, sliced thin

Warm Red Cabbage Salad ingredients

⅔ cup oil-cured olives, pitted and chopped

¾ pound feta cheese, crumbled

1 cup unsalted pistachio nuts, toasted

Asian Ginger Cabbage

I n this Asian interpretation, soy sauce is used in place of the vinegar in the basic recipe and sesame oil instead of the olive oil.

Add the carrots, pepper, garlic, ginger and green onions to the cabbage. Cook in sesame oil according to the directions for Warm Red Cabbage Salad, adding the soy sauce, water chestnuts, mint, cilantro and red pepper flakes just before it is done. Season with salt and pepper and mix well. Garnish with the roasted peanuts.

Makes 6 to 8 servings.

1 cup carrots, slivered

1 green pepper, slivered

3 cloves garlic, minced

5-inch piece ginger, peeled and minced

1 cup green onions, diagonal cut

1 head red cabbage, sliced very thin

2 red onions, sliced thin

Sesame oil

¼ cup soy sauce

½ cup water chestnuts, diced

½ cup mint, chopped

½ cup cilantro, chopped

Pinch red pepper flakes

Salt and pepper, to taste

1 cup peanuts, roasted

COOK'S NOTE:

If you like hot food, add 2 or 3 jalapeno peppers, minced.

Composed Salad of Noodles and Vegetables
with Peanut Dressing

1 pound thin noodles,
   preferably Chinese or
   Japanese
1 bunch asparagus, 1-
   inch diagonal cut
2 carrots, slivered

DRESSING
2 cups coconut milk
½ cup chunky peanut
   butter
4 cloves garlic, minced
5-inch piece ginger,
   peeled and minced
1 tsp. each ground black
   pepper, coriander,
   caraway seed and
   dried red pepper
Juice from 1 lime
½ cup soy sauce

1 small head red
   cabbage, shredded
   fine
1 cup cilantro, chopped
1 bunch green onions,
   1-inch diagonal cut
1 handful snow peas,
   slivered
1 handful bean sprouts
4 small pickling
   cucumbers, or 2
   medium English
   cucumbers, peeled
   and diagonally sliced
1 bunch red radishes,
   tops intact
1 large red pepper,
   julienne

*T*his salad offers something for everyone and will probably encourage lasting cravings for peanut sauce, if you
or your guests haven't already developed that condition.

Cook noodles in salted boiling water until firm but tender.
Drain and cool. Blanch the asparagus and carrots separately.

   To make the dressing, in a small saucepan heat the coconut milk and the peanut butter and stir until smooth. Add
the remaining ingredients, mix well and cook over medium
heat until thick and smooth. Taste and adjust seasoning; add
more soy sauce for a saltier taste and more red pepper for a
hotter bite. Allow the dressing to cool.

   To arrange the salad, make a bed of red cabbage. Dress
the noodles with ½ the peanut dressing and place in the center of the platter. Garnish with the chopped cilantro and the
green onions. Arrange the vegetables in small clusters
around the noodles, alternating colors, red-green-white. Pass
the remaining dressing.

   Makes 6 to 8 servings.

COOK'S NOTE:

You may want to serve hard boiled eggs as garnish or Five-
Spice Tea Cooked Eggs (see page 37).

Warm Greens
with Smoked Mozzarella and Yams

*T*his comforting salad has some surprise taste treats. The bitter greens form a perfect canvas for smoked cheese and sweet yams. Figure one large handful of assorted greens per person for a medium-sized salad.

Cut the cheese into small cubes. If the cheese is soft, use a serrated knife for easier cutting. Cook the yams in the olive oil, butter and spices over moderate heat until golden brown. Add lemon juice and season with salt and pepper. Set aside.

To make the salad, place the greens and the vinegars in a large bowl. Heat the fruity olive oil and garlic in a small skillet over moderate heat. When the oil *just* begins to smoke and the garlic is golden, carefully pour the hot oil into the side of the bowl containing the greens. Quickly toss the greens in the hot oil, incorporating the vinegar as well. Place the wilted greens on plates and garnish with the cheese and the fried yams.

Makes 6 to 8 servings.

1 pound smoked mozzarella or any other naturally smoked cheese

3 medium yams, medium dice

¼ cup olive oil

2 Tb. unsalted butter

1 tsp. each coriander, nutmeg, mace, paprika

Juice from lemon

Salt and white pepper, to taste

Assorted greens (see COOK'S NOTE)

Large splash each of balsamic, red wine and sherry vinegar

½ to ¾ cup fruity olive oil

2 cloves garlic, minced

COOK'S NOTE:

Mild greens combined with the more assertive bitter greens make for a flavorful and interesting combination of tastes. Choose from any of these bitter greens: frisée, escarole, radicchio, mustard greens, dandelion greens, curly endive, watercress and rocket (arugula). Choose one or two of these mild lettuces to round out the salad: hearts of romaine, spinach, curly green leaf, baby limestone or hearts of butter lettuce.

Asparagus and Summer Vegetable Salad

I can't think of a better way to indulge in the bounty of summer. This salad combines all the best from a summer garden. Fresh, colorful vegetables burst with flavor and the essence of the season. A delicious chilled salad for those steamy, sultry nights.

2 small bunches asparagus, 1-inch diagonal cut

1 large carrot, small dice

1 cup shelled English peas

3 ears sweet white corn, shaved

2 red peppers, small dice

1 small yellow squash, small dice

1 pint cherry tomatoes, halved, or Sweet 100's (see COOK'S NOTE)

1 large avocado

Juice from 2 limes

Zest from 1 lime

Zest from 1 lemon

2 cups Basic Mayonnaise (see page 28)

Salt and pepper, to taste

2 heads butter lettuce

1 cup shelled pistachio nuts

COOK'S NOTE:

Sweet 100's are a very sweet and very small tomato variety.

Blanch the asparagus, carrot, and peas separately. Combine blanched vegetables, corn, peppers, squash and tomatoes in a large bowl.

In a blender puree the avocado with the lime juice. Add the puréed avocado and the zest to the mayonnaise. Season with salt and pepper.

Gently fold the dressing into the vegetables and mix well. Taste and adjust seasoning. Place on a bed of lettuce and garnish with the pistachios.

Makes 6 to 8 servings.

Warm Grilled Potato Salad

A zesty, full-flavored warm salad, perfect for hot summer afternoons and nights. Light the coals and forget about standing in a hot kitchen, stirring large pots of stuff. This salad combines the flavors and tastes of some of my favorite foods.

Prepare a charcoal grill.

Combine the oil, chili powder, cumin, coriander, bitters, black pepper and salt. Brush the sliced potatoes with the seasoned oil. Grill the potatoes over medium hot coals, basting often with the oil until the potatoes are crisp and golden brown—not black! Remove potatoes from the grill and set aside.

Combine the balsamic vinegar with the mayonnaise. Place the greens on plates. Cut the grilled potatoes into cubes, place in a large bowl with the onions, cheese, peppers and sun-dried tomatoes. Toss with the dressing and garnish with the capers. Offer cracked black pepper.

Makes 6 to 8 servings.

1 cup olive oil
1 Tb. prepared chili powder
1 Tb. cumin seed, ground
1 Tb. coriander, ground
Dash of Angostura bitters
1 tsp. black pepper
1 tsp. salt
4 large baking potatoes, sliced ½-inch thick, lengthwise
½ cup balsamic vinegar
1½ cups mayonnaise
1 to 2 bunches mustard greens, depending on the size, washed and torn into 2-inch pieces
2 small red onions, sliced thin
¾ to 1 pound smoked mozzarella, or any naturally smoked cheese, medium dice
2 green peppers, julienne
⅓ cup sun-dried tomatoes, fine chop
¼ cup capers, for garnish

COOK'S NOTE:

This is a warm salad. Be sure to have all the ingredients ready so that when the potatoes come off the grill you can serve them right away.

Warm Spicy Eggplant Salad
with Sesame Noodles

Don't let the long list of ingredients scare you off! Many of the ingredients are spices or "splashes" of this or that—it's playful work. As with most Asian cooking, a great portion of the work is in the preparation, while the actual cooking time is minimal.

NOODLES

1½ ounces tree ear mushrooms, or any other Asian dried mushroom

1 pound thin noodles, preferably buckwheat or wholewheat

⅔ cup sesame oil

2 cloves garlic, minced

3 Tb. soy sauce

3 Tb. mushroom soy sauce

Splash teriyaki sauce

¼ cup seasoned rice wine vinegar

½ cup sesame seed, toasted

1 yellow onion, sliced very thin

1 bunch green onions, chopped small

1 cup cilantro, chopped coarse

Soak the dried mushrooms in warm water for about 1 hour. Slice very thin.

Cook the noodles in salted boiling water until just tender. Drain.

Heat the sesame oil and garlic in a small pan. When warm, pour over the noodles. To the noodles add the three sauces and the vinegar. Taste and adjust seasoning. Add the remaining noodle ingredients, mix well and set aside.

Cook the eggplant, onion, garlic, ginger, red pepper flakes and five-spice powder in the oils over moderate heat until soft and juicy. Add the tomatoes, cook over high heat for 1 or 2 minutes, reduce heat and add the remaining ingredients. Cook over moderate heat for about 10 minutes. Taste and adjust seasoning.

Arrange the noodles on individual plates or one large platter, spoon the warm eggplant over the noodles. Garnish with sprigs of cilantro. Serve immediately.

Makes 6 to 8 servings.

EGGPLANT MIXTURE

4 Japanese eggplants, cut into ½-inch wide pieces

1 large yellow onion, wedge cut

6 cloves garlic, minced

¼ cup minced fresh ginger

1 scant Tb. red pepper flakes

1 Tb. Chinese five-spice powder (see page 30)

¼ cup sesame oil

¼ cup peanut oil

2 medium tomatoes, medium dice

⅓ cup soy sauce

3 Tb. black bean vinegar

3 Tb. seasoned rice wine vinegar

2 Tb. brown sugar

2 Tb. mushroom soy sauce

Cilantro, for garnish

Romaine
with Feta, Figs and Pine Nuts

A simple salad that sparkles with flavor and requires no advance preparation. Romaine lettuce provides a perfect crispy and juicy crunch to go along with the tender figs, toasty pine nuts and rich feta cheese.

¾ cup pine nuts, toasted

1 red onion, sliced paper thin

1 very large bunch or 2 medium bunches romaine lettuce, chopped into 1-inch pieces

Sherry Vinaigrette (see page 51)

¾ pound feta cheese, crumbled

10 black Mission figs, sliced into thin rounds

Freshly cracked black pepper

Toss the pine nuts and red onion with the greens. Pour some vinaigrette over the greens and toss well. Arrange on plates, top with a little feta cheese and garnish with the sliced figs. Sprinkle with a generous amount of freshly cracked black pepper.

Makes 6 servings.

Spaghetti Squash Salad

A unique salad combining sweet currants, juicy oranges, ginger and nutty squash. The golden strands of tasty squash are the perfect base for the light citrus vinaigrette.

Macerate the currants in the rum and orange juice for at least 2 hours.

Preheat oven to 400° F.

Bake the spaghetti squash in a large shallow baking dish with a little water, cut side down until *just* tender when pierced with a fork. Remove from the oven and cool. Remove squash from the "shell" (see COOK'S NOTE) and set aside in a bowl.

Drain the currants, add half of the rum-orange juice marinade to the squash and gently mix so as not to break the strands. Combine the currants, peppers, ginger and oranges in a bowl. Dress with half of the Four-Citrus Vinaigrette. Arrange some squash on each plate and top with the dressed vegetables. Garnish each serving with the toasted walnuts and drizzle the remaining vinaigrette over the salads. Serve immediately.

Makes 6 servings.

1 cup currants
½ cup light rum
½ cup orange juice
Large spaghetti squash, halved and seeds removed
1 large red pepper, small dice
1 green pepper, small dice
3-inch piece fresh ginger, peeled and sliced paper thin
2 blood oranges or sweet oranges, sectioned
Four-Citrus Vinaigrette (see page 52)
1 cup toasted walnuts

COOK'S NOTE:

Spaghetti squash is a large winter vegetable, shaped like a football and with a yellow outer skin. Its deep golden flesh has a texture similar to that of spaghetti. When cooked properly the flesh retains its strandlike shape. To remove the "strands" of squash, loosen the squash from the outer shell with a butter knife, then use a fork to lift the flesh out. (See illustration at left.)

Stocks and Soups

Stocks

A flavorful stock is one of the basic components of good cooking, and oftentimes a stock is the backbone of a dish. Care and attention should be taken when making these flavorful liquids. A watery, bland stock will only give you watery, bland soups and watery, bland sauces.

If you cook on a regular basis, save your vegetable trimmings: carrot ends, onion ends, bean trimmings, corn cobs, tomatoes, potato trimmings and the like. Careful, though! A vegetable stock is not a garbage can. Use only fresh, wholesome vegetables and trimmings. Avoid celery leaves and eggplant, which cause bitterness, and all vegetables belonging to the cabbage family, such as broccoli, cauliflower, and brussel sprouts.

Basic Vegetable Stock

Use this stock for almost any soup, sauce or cooking liquid. It is the basic stock, meaning no one flavor dominates. The quantity of any vegetable may be doubled or tripled to suit a given recipe. For example, if you are making a cream of zucchini soup, you could double the amount of zucchini called for in the basic vegetable stock and decrease the amount of carrots.

Rough chop all the vegetables. Place all ingredients in a large stockpot, bring to a boil and skim any foam (impurities) off the surface. Reduce heat and simmer, uncovered, for 3 to 4 hours. Be sure to stir the stock once in a while. Strain and cool before refrigerating. The stock can be reduced to intensify the flavors. Stock will keep for 1 week in the refrigerator, or 2 to 3 months in the freezer.

Makes about 2 gallons.

4 onions
5 celery ribs
4 carrots
4 whole tomatoes
4 zucchini or summer
  squash
2 corn cobs, if available
2 potatoes
2 bell peppers, any
  color
1 head garlic, separated
½ pound string beans
½ pound mushrooms
2 bunches parsley
4 bay leaves
Small handful black
  peppercorns
1½-2 gallons cold water

Mushroom Stock

4 ribs celery
4 tomatoes
4 onions
3 carrots
2 potatoes
2 heads garlic,
   separated
2 pounds mushrooms
6 ounces dried shiitake
   mushrooms
4 ounces dried porcini
   mushrooms
1 bunch parsley
4 sprigs thyme
4 bay leaves
3 Tb. black peppercorns
1½-2 gallons cold water

Rough chop all the vegetables except the mushrooms. Place all the ingredients in a large stockpot and bring to a boil. Reduce the heat and simmer, uncovered, for 3 to 4 hours. Strain the stock and squeeze the juices out of the vegetables and dried mushrooms— these vital liquids contain a lot of flavor. For a more intense flavor, reduce 1½ gallons of stock to 1 gallon.

Makes about 2 gallons.

COOK'S NOTE:

Mushroom soy sauce, available at Asian grocery stores or Asian sections of supermarkets, is an excellent flavor booster for mushroom recipes. Add some if the stock needs a little intensity, but remember the soy is quite salty.

Tomato Stock

28-ounce can whole
   tomatoes
8 whole fresh tomatoes
4 onions
4 zucchini
4 ribs celery
1 pound string beans
3 carrots
8 cloves garlic
1 bunch parsley
4 bay leaves
3 sprigs oregano
3 Tb. black peppercorns
1½-2 gallons cold water

Rough chop all the vegetables. Place all the ingredients in a large stockpot and bring to a boil. Reduce heat and simmer, uncovered, 3 to 4 hours. Be sure to stir the pot from time to time. Strain the stock, squeezing the juices from the vegetables. The stock may be reduced to intensify the flavor.

Makes about 2 gallons.

Soups

I like to make large, even copious amounts of soup. This habit partly stems from cooking in restaurants, standing over huge stockpots filled with gallons of soup and still wondering, "Will it be enough?" Okay, so few home cooks *need* 20 gallons of soup, but if you're going to spend the time making a stock, cutting up all sorts of vegetables, why not chop a few extra carrots and onions and *really* have some soup? Soup is meant for groups, then leftovers. Soup gets better the second and third day. Soup can be reheated with ease and grace. Most soup can even be frozen. Soup is the perfect food for lots of people. Soup can be the ideal meal! Soup, soup, soup.

You can throw practically anything in the soup pot as long as it tastes good on its own. Use fresh, wholesome produce, rich stocks, handsome herbs, good wines, sherries and ports, flavorful olive oils, and top-notch dairy products. Have fun. There aren't any strict rules when it comes to soup making.

Some soups may be served as the main dish, depending on how filling they are or how hungry your guests are! Generally speaking, soups starring the heartier ingredients, such as beans, potatoes and dairy products, make a meal in themselves. A pleasant meal for guests and family could include an appetizer, followed by a salad and then a soup course as the entrée. Or offer a soup course to add a touch of elegance to a somewhat plain dinner. Be sure to have some bread, tortillas, rolls or crackers to go with the soup.

Spicy Eggplant Soup
with Rouille

*T*his soup is good for the dead of winter because it is hearty, thick and spicy and sticks to the ribs. Fresh tomatoes are difficult to find during the cold months—and if you do find some, you often wish you hadn't bothered to look. This soup works quite well using canned tomatoes.

2 large eggplants
Olive oil
Salt and pepper
2 large yellow onions, rough chop
4 jalapeno peppers, rough chop
5 cloves garlic, chopped
8 cardamom pods, ground
2 Tb. cumin seed, ground
1 Tb. black pepper
¼ cup sesame oil
2 Tb. Curry Oil (recipe follows)
28-ounce can whole tomatoes
15-ounce can tomato sauce
10 cups Vegetable Stock (see page 69)
½ cup mushroom soy sauce
¼ cup dry sherry
3 Tb. sherry vinegar
Rouille (recipe follows), for garnish

Preheat oven to 400° F.

Halve the eggplants lengthwise, brush the cut side with the olive oil and sprinkle with salt and pepper. Bake cut side down on sheet pans until soft. Cool, remove pulp and discard the skin.

Sauté the onions, jalapeno peppers, garlic, and ground spices in the sesame and curry oils. Add the tomato products and cook over high heat for 1 to 2 minutes. Add eggplant pulp, stock and remaining ingredients. Cook over moderate heat for 5 to 10 minutes, remove from heat and cool slightly. Puree in a blender until smooth. Heat pureed soup over low heat. When hot, taste and adjust seasoning. If the soup is too thick, thin it with a little stock or water. Garnish with Rouille (see COOK'S NOTE).

Makes 10 to 12 servings.

CURRY OIL

Bruise the spices by partially grinding in a spice grinder or with a mortar and pestle. Simmer the spices in the oil for 30 minutes. Strain the oil and keep refrigerated. Discard the spices.

    Makes 1½ cups.

6 Tb. coriander
6 Tb. cumin seed
4 Tb. fennel seed
2 Tb. fenugreek
2 Tb. black peppercorns
2 Tb. turmeric
10 to 15 cardamom pods
5 star anise
2 dried hot chiles
2 tsp. mustard seeds
1½ cups peanut or
    safflower oil

ROUILLE

My version of rouille has no eggs or bread. It is quite simple.

Soak the chiles in water for 2 to 4 hours.

    Drain the chiles; discard the stems and seeds. In a blender puree the ancho chiles, roasted red pepper, garlic, and sugar with the balsamic vinegar. Thin with a little water if necessary. Taste and adjust for salt.

    Makes about 1½ cups.

3 to 4 ancho chiles (see
    COOK'S NOTE)
1 roasted red pepper
2 cloves garlic
Pinch of sugar
Splash of balsamic
    vinegar
Salt, to taste

COOK'S NOTE:

To garnish the soup, swirl the rouille on the surface of the individual servings, making a simple design.

    Ancho chile peppers can be found in Latin American markets. The taste is deep and spicy, but not too hot. Like all chiles, the seeds and skins are the hottest part. Use gloves when handling hot peppers and avoid contact with eyes and sensitive skin.

Coconut Curry Vegetable Soup

2 Tb. coriander

1 Tb. cumin seed

1 Tb. black peppercorns

1 tsp. whole caraway seed

1 tsp. fenugreek

1 tsp. anise seed

2 tsp. turmeric

1 tsp. whole cloves

5 cardamom pods

Pinch each nutmeg, cinnamon and mace

4 dried red chiles

⅔ cup ghee (see page 19)

2 large yellow onions, medium dice

6 cloves garlic, minced

5-inch piece ginger, peeled and minced

3 red jalapeno peppers, minced

4 Tb. all-purpose flour

3 large white potatoes, medium dice

2 large carrots, roll cut

6 cups Vegetable Stock (page 69)

4 cups coconut milk (see COOK'S NOTE)

1 large summer squash, medium dice

5 tomatoes, medium dice

2 bunches spinach, cleaned and cut into 2-inch pieces

1 cup cilantro, rough chop

Salt and pepper, to taste

*D*on't be scared off by the long list of ingredients. This soup is easy to make and so delicious! The spices are deep and complex, hot and spicy, with the sweetness of the coconut milk balancing the sensations and flavors perfectly. If you are a newcomer to the delights of coconut milk, I'm sure you will really enjoy this unique taste treat.

Grind all the spices and dried chiles. Place in a small skillet and toast over low heat until the spices become aromatic and their fragrance fills the air. *Do not let the spices burn.* Remove from the skillet.

Melt the ghee in a large pot. Sauté the onions, garlic, ginger and jalapeno peppers in the ghee over high heat for 1 to 2 minutes. Reduce heat, add the flour, and cook until the onions are soft. Add the potatoes and carrots and sauté for 1 to 2 minutes. Add the stock and cook over high heat until the potatoes and carrots are almost done, about 7 to 10 minutes, stirring often. Add the coconut milk and squash, reduce heat, and cook until all the vegetables are tender but not soft or mushy. Just before serving, add the diced tomatoes, chopped spinach and cilantro. Taste and adjust seasoning for salt and pepper.

Makes 10 to 12 servings.

COOK'S NOTE:

Use canned unsweetened coconut milk. This specialty item can be found in most Asian and Latin American grocery stores and in some major supermarket chains.

Cream of Summer Squash
with Pesto

*T*his soup is smooth, silky and elegant. It is easy to prepare, inexpensive and makes a very dramatic presentation with the contrasting swirl of bright green pesto.

Cook the onions, Five-pepper Mix and garlic in the butter
until onions are soft. Add the squash and cook for 2 to 3 minutes. Add the stock and bring to a boil. Reduce heat and simmer until the squash is tender but not mushy. Cool slightly.
In a blender puree the mixture. Return to the pot and heat.
Add the cream, sherry and salt and pepper. Taste and adjust
seasoning. Garnish with pesto (see COOK'S NOTE).
    Makes 10 to 12 servings.

2 large yellow onions,
  rough chop
1 Tb. Five-pepper Mix,
  ground (page 29)
3 cloves garlic, chopped
¼ pound unsalted
  butter
2 pounds yellow squash,
  chopped medium
10 cups Vegetable Stock
  (page 69)
1 pint heavy cream
Splash sherry
Salt and pepper, to taste
Pesto, for garnish
  (recipe follows)

PESTO

Puree all ingredients in a blender. Add a little water if the
mixture clumps up. Taste and adjust for salt and pepper.
    Makes about 1½ cups.

2 large bunches fresh
  basil, leaves only
2 cloves garlic
⅓ cup pine nuts
¼ cup Parmesan
  cheese, freshly grated
1 cup olive oil
Salt and white pepper,
  to taste

COOK'S NOTE:

To garnish the soup, swirl the pesto on the surface of the individual servings, making a simple but elegant design. Store
leftover pesto in a small jar or bowl and cover with a thin film
of olive oil. It will keep for about 2 to 3 weeks in the refrigerator.

Wild and Domestic Mushroom Soup
with Orzo

T*his soup, "meaty" with the essence of mushroom, will satisfy and soothe the most insistent carnivores.*

4 ounces dried shiitake mushrooms

4 ounces dried porcini mushrooms

2 ounces dried cèpes

2 large onions, medium dice

6 cloves garlic, minced

¼ pound unsalted butter

Olive oil

1 pound domestic brown or button mushrooms, sliced medium

⅓ pound porcini mushrooms, sliced ½ inch thick

⅓ pound Italian field mushrooms, cleaned thoroughly and sliced ½ inch thick

1 cup dry red wine, for deglazing

⅓ pound shiitake mushrooms, stemmed and sliced ½ inch thick

⅓ pound morels, cut into ½-inch rounds

½ cup mushroom soy sauce

1 tsp. dry thyme

1 tsp. dry sage

1 cup port

12 cups strong Mushroom Stock (page 70)

½ pound orzo or riso (rice-shaped pasta)

Salt and pepper, to taste

Simmer the dried mushrooms in a about 1 quart of water for 1½ hours. Cool. Strain the liquid through 2 layers of cheese-cloth, squeezing the juice from the mushrooms. Rinse the mushrooms under running water, cleaning any grit and dirt as you go. Chop the cleaned mushrooms and set aside. Reduce the mushroom liquid by half. Set aside.

Sauté the onions and garlic in 4 tablespoons butter over low heat in a large stockpot.

Meanwhile, in a a large sauté pan, heat a little butter and some olive oil to coat. Sear the domestic, porcini and Italian field mushrooms over high heat until golden brown. Deglaze the pan with a little red wine. Cook the shiitakes and the morels in a little stock. (Be sure to stir the onions once in a while.) Combine all the cooked mushrooms in a bowl and season with the mushroom soy sauce, thyme and sage.

When the onions and garlic are soft, add the port, and cook over high heat for 3 to 4 minutes. Add the mushroom stock and cook over high heat for 5 to 6 minutes, stirring often. Reduce heat, add the orzo and simmer until pasta is almost done. Add the dried mushrooms and the cooked fresh mushrooms. Heat through and taste. Adding mushroom soy instead of salt will enrich the flavor.

Makes 10 to 12 servings.

COOK'S NOTE:

Please read my pointers on cooking mushrooms (page 19). In this recipe the shiitakes and the morels are delicate, and the rest are sturdy, hearty mushrooms. If wild and imported mushrooms are unavailable, make substitutions. Porta Bella, chanterelles and oyster mushrooms are also wonderful. Just be sure to really clean the mushrooms well, with a damp cloth—not in the sink with water! You may want to garnish this soup with grated Asiago or Parmesan cheese.

Four-Onion and Roasted Garlic Soup

Easy, delicious and simple, the roasted garlic adds depth, richness and a unique flavor. Garlic lovers will probably move in with you—permanently—after indulging in this bit of heaven.

Preheat oven to 400° F.

Coat the cut side of the garlic with some olive oil, place cut side down in a small baking pan with about ¼ inch of water. Bake until the garlic is soft, about 40 minutes to 1 hour. When cool, squeeze the garlic from the skin, taking care not to let any of the papery thin skin fall into the garlic. Set aside.

Cook the yellow and red onions in the butter and some olive oil over high heat for 3 to 4 minutes, reduce heat and add the herbs. Cook over low heat until golden brown and caramelized, 30 to 40 minutes. Add the boiling onions, leeks, and minced garlic and cook over high heat for 1 to 2 minutes. Add the port and reduce heat. Cook until all the onions are soft. Add the roasted garlic, mushroom soy and bitters, and stir well. Slowly add the mushroom stock, stirring constantly so the roasted garlic makes a paste. Taste and adjust seasoning. Garnish if desired with Parmesan, herbs or croutons.

Makes 8 to 10 servings.

3 whole heads garlic, stem end cut ¼ inch (to expose the flesh of each garlic clove)

Olive oil

3 large yellow onions, ½-inch thick wedge cut

2 red onions, ½-inch thick wedge cut

3 Tb. unsalted butter

1 tsp. dry thyme

1 tsp. dry oregano

1 tsp. dry basil

10 to 15 boiling or pearl onions, root end trimmed and peeled

1 very large or 2 medium leeks, sliced ¼ to ½ inch wide

3 cloves garlic, minced

½ cup port

⅓ to ½ cup mushroom soy sauce

Dash Angostura bitters

1 gallon strong Mushroom Stock (page 70)

Salt and pepper, to taste

OPTIONAL GARNISH

½ cup Parmesan cheese, freshly grated

½ cup minced fresh herbs

10 or 12 croutons

Three-Bean and Potato Soup

This soup has many tastes, textures and colors. It tastes even better on the second or third day.

½ cup white beans
½ cup black beans
½ cup red beans (not kidney beans)
Salt and pepper, to taste
2 large yellow onions, medium dice
6 cloves garlic, minced
2 tsp. dry thyme
1 Tb. dry oregano
2 tsp. dry basil
2 tsp. fennel seed, ground
2 tsp. cumin seed, ground
4 bay leaves
½ cup fruity olive oil
2 red potatoes, medium dice
2 yams, medium dice
1 carrot, small dice
4 tomatoes, peeled, seeded and chopped medium, or 28-ounce can chopped tomatoes
12 cups Tomato Stock (page 70)
½ cup mushroom soy sauce
1 handful mustard greens, chopped into 2-inch pieces
1 handful spinach, chopped into 2-inch pieces
Salt and pepper, to taste

Soak the beans overnight, keeping each color separate, in three times their volume of water.

Cook the beans separately (see COOK'S NOTE) in their soaking water for 45 minutes to 1 hour. When the beans are done, season lightly with salt and pepper. Set aside in their cooking liquid.

Cook the onions, garlic, herbs and spices in the olive oil until the onions are soft. Add the potatoes, yams, carrots and tomatoes and cook over high heat for 2 to 3 minutes. Add the tomato stock, bring to a boil, reduce heat, add mushroom soy and simmer until the vegetables are tender. When the vegetables are almost done, add the beans and their cooking liquids, stir well and cook for 5 to 10 minutes before tasting. Season to taste with salt and pepper. Just before serving, add the chopped greens and stir well.

Makes 10 to 12 servings.

COOK'S NOTE:

Sort beans for small rocks and pebbles. Always rinse before cooking. Simmer beans uncovered and *unsalted*—salting and boiling make them tough.

Tomato and Cheddar Cheese Soup

This soup is heartwarming and rich. It is so easy to make, I know you will never eat canned tomato soup again!

Cook the onions, garlic, herbs and spices in the butter in a large pot over low heat. When the onions are soft, add the tomatoes and cook over high heat for 2 to 3 minutes. Add the red wine and continue cooking over high heat for 5 minutes, stirring often. Add the stock and simmer for 10 to 15 minutes. Remove from the heat and cool slightly. In a blender puree the mixture until smooth. Strain the soup through a fine wire mesh colander or screen to remove the tomato skins and seeds. Return to the pot and heat. Add the cream and sherry. Taste and season with salt and pepper. Just before serving, add the grated cheese, a little at a time, stirring to incorporate the cheese into the soup. Serve immediately with desired garnish.

Makes 10 to 12 servings.

2 medium red onions, coarse chop

4 cloves garlic, minced

1 tsp. dry thyme

1 tsp. whole allspice, ground

½ tsp. cayenne (see COOK'S NOTE)

¼ pound unsalted butter

1½ pounds fresh tomatoes, rough chop, or 4 cups canned tomatoes, chopped

¾ cup red wine

10 to 12 cups Tomato Stock (page 70)

1 pint heavy cream

Splash of dry sherry

¾ pound sharp Cheddar cheese, grated fine

Salt and pepper, to taste

1 cup minced chives, or croutons, for garnish (optional)

COOK'S NOTE:

If you like really hot food, just increase the cayenne or add a dash of Tabasco to each bowl.

Sweet Corn Soup
with Chile Pepper

*T*his is a wonderful way to enjoy the pleasures of corn when summer seduces us into overindulging in the delights of almost everything.

1 gallon corn stock (see COOK'S NOTE)

2 large yellow onions, medium chop

3 cloves garlic, minced

Pinch cardamom, ground

¼ pound unsalted butter

10 to 12 ears sweet corn, shaved

1 large yellow squash, medium dice

1 pint heavy cream

Salt and white pepper, to taste

6 California chiles (long, narrow and green, slightly hot), roasted, peeled and seeded

GARNISH

2 roasted red peppers, peeled and seeded

Splash balsamic vinegar

Salt and white pepper, to taste

Reduce corn stock to 10 cups. Set aside.

Cook onions, garlic and cardamom in butter until onions are soft. Add corn kernels and yellow squash and cook over medium heat for 5 to 10 minutes, depending on the sweetness and toughness of the corn. Add the corn stock, stir well and cook for 3 to 4 minutes. In a blender puree the soup. (The soup will not be completely smooth, even after pureeing.) Force the soup through a wire mesh, extracting as much liquid as possible. Return the soup to the pot and boil for 5 to 10 minutes; this reduction intensifies the flavors. Reduce the heat and add the cream, salt and pepper.

Dice the roasted chiles and add to the soup. Stir well, taste and adjust seasoning.

Puree the roasted red peppers, balsamic vinegar, salt and pepper in a blender. Thin the puree with a little water if necessary. Swirl a simple design of puree on the surface of each individual bowl of soup.

Makes 10 to 12 servings.

COOK'S NOTE:

To make corn stock: Make the Basic Vegetable Stock (page 69) but omit the mushrooms and tomatoes, and substitute 10 shaved corn cobs, halved, and 2 whole corn cobs, halved.

Cream of Red Pepper and Tomato Soup

*R*ed, intense and spicy. This soup is red. It's one of my favorites. The spices make for an intriguing and satisfying soup.

Soak the ancho chiles in water to cover for 4 to 6 hours or until they are soft and pliable. Remove stems and seeds.

Cook onions, garlic, red peppers, and spices in butter over high heat for 3 to 4 minutes, stirring constantly. Add the tomatoes, sherry and balsamic vinegar and stir well. Add the tomato stock, bring to a boil and remove from heat.

Puree the soup with the ancho chiles in a blender until smooth. Return to the pot and bring to a boil. Add the cream, sugar, salt and pepper. Heat through. Taste and adjust seasoning. Garnish as desired.

Makes 10 to 12 servings.

1 or 2 ancho chiles
2 medium red onions, rough chop
4 cloves garlic, minced
6 large red peppers, rough chop
1 tsp. cumin seed, ground
2 tsp. Five-pepper Mix, ground (page 29)
⅓ pound unsalted butter
6 medium tomatoes, or 28-ounce can tomatoes, peeled, seeded and rough chop
¼ cup sherry
¼ cup balsamic vinegar
8 to 10 cups Tomato Stock (page 70)
1 pint heavy cream
1 Tb. sugar
Salt and pepper, to taste
Crème fraîche or sour cream, for garnish (optional)
Cilantro or fresh chives, for garnish (optional)

COOK'S NOTE:

Crème fraîche makes a soothing and handsome garnish for this soup. If crème fraîche is not available, use sour cream thinned with a little water. Cilantro or chives also make a stunning and delicious final touch.

Cauliflower Soup
with Melted Gouda Croutons

I f you're not crazy about cauliflower, or haven't found an interesting recipe for cauliflower soup, try this one. I promise you will become a believer after sipping the rich flavors of this soup.

2 medium onions, rough chop
5 cloves garlic, minced
1 Tb. coriander, ground
1½ tsp. caraway seed, ground
½ tsp. cayenne
⅓ pound unsalted butter
6 cups rough-chopped cauliflower, core included
1 carrot, coarse chop
¼ cup sherry
12 cups Basic Vegetable Stock (page 69)
Salt and pepper, to taste
3 cloves garlic, minced
½ cup olive oil
1 thin baguette
½ pound imported Gouda cheese

Cook the onions, garlic and spices in the butter over medium heat until the onions are soft. Add the cauliflower, carrot and sherry and cook over high heat for 2 to 3 minutes, stirring all the while. Add the stock and bring to a boil. Reduce heat and simmer until the cauliflower is tender but not mushy. Cool slightly. Puree in a blender until smooth. Return to the pot and bring pureed soup to a boil. Reduce heat, add salt and pepper, and simmer for 10 to 15 minutes. Taste and adjust seasoning.

Preheat oven to 350° F.

Combine the garlic with the olive oil. Slice the baguette into rounds ¼ inch thick, brush with the garlic oil and bake croutons until golden brown. Slice the cheese to fit the croutons. Just before serving the soup, place the cheese-topped croutons under the broiler and heat until the cheese melts. Place one on the surface of each individual bowl.

Makes 10 to 12 servings.

Appetizers

Some of the appetizers in this chapter are complex, hearty and filling, while others are simple and elegant. All can also be served—in larger portions—as main courses or serve several appetizers instead of one large entrée. The assortment of tastes, textures and cuisines will please everyone, especially if you prepare a good salad and pour lots of wine or other beverages.

Eggplant Rollatini
with Roasted Red Pepper Sauce

1 large yellow onion, small dice

6 cloves garlic, minced

¼ cup olive oil

2 large zucchini, small dice

1 pound fresh ricotta cheese

½ pound mozzarella cheese, grated

¼ pound Asiago cheese, grated fine

¼ pound Gruyère cheese, grated fine

1 tsp. red pepper flakes

½ tsp. cardamom pods, ground

½ tsp. nutmeg

Pinch mace

½ cup mixed fresh herbs, minced (see page 12)

Salt and pepper, to taste

2 large eggplant, sliced ¼ to ½ inch thick

3 eggs, lightly beaten

1½ to 2 cups fine bread crumbs

Vegetable oil, for frying

Roasted Red Pepper Sauce (recipe follows)

Flat leaf parsley, for garnish

3 roasted red peppers, peeled, seeded and stemmed

3 Tb. balsamic vinegar

Fresh Tomato Sauce (page 28)

This seductively savory dish will last in the memories of those who indulge in its round and appealing flavors. The eggplant is delicately fried, tender and moist, not rubbery or bland. The preparation of the eggplant, not to mention the lavish combination of flavors in this dish could convert even the most stubborn eggplant-haters.

Cook the onion and garlic in the olive oil until the onion is soft. Add the zucchini and cook until the zucchini is bright green and tender, but not mushy. Set aside to cool.

Combine the ricotta, other cheeses, spices, herbs, salt and pepper, mix well, taste and adjust seasoning. When onion-zucchini mixture is cool add to cheese mixture. Set aside.

Dip a piece of eggplant in the beaten eggs, then coat with bread crumbs. Set aside on a sheet pan. Repeat with the remaining eggplant slices. Refrigerate for 20 to 30 minutes.

Heat 2 inches of vegetable oil in a skillet. When hot but not smoking, add as many pieces of eggplant as will fit without crowding. Cook over moderate heat until golden brown, flip and cook other side until golden brown. Drain on paper towels. Cook all the eggplant this way. If the oil becomes dirty or smells burned, discard and start with new oil.

Preheat oven to 350° F.

To assemble, place about 2 tablespoons of filling at one end of a slice of eggplant and roll the eggplant around the filling. Repeat with remaining eggplant and filling. Bake seam side down for 15 to 20 minutes, or until warmed through. Serve immediately with Roasted Red Pepper Sauce and garnish with a sprig of parsley.

Makes about 8 servings.

ROASTED RED PEPPER SAUCE

Puree the peppers and balsamic vinegar in a blender until smooth. Add to the tomato sauce. Taste and adjust seasoning. Serve warm. Makes 3 to 4 cups.

Wild & Domestic Mushroom Ragout
with Polenta Shapes

*T*his *earthy and hearty dish is perfect any time of year, but cold weather always inspires me to indulge in the delectable combination of creamy polenta with assorted flavorful mushrooms.*

Make the Basic Polenta and just before the polenta is done, add the cheeses, mix well and pour into a 9 by 12-inch baking dish. Refrigerate for 4 to 6 hours.

Cook onions and garlic in 3 tablespoons butter over moderate heat until the onions are soft. Set aside in a large bowl.

Cook the assorted mushrooms separately in olive oil. When each batch of mushrooms is done, remove from the pan, set aside and return pan to the heat. Add a large splash of wine to the pan. Scrape the browned bits of mushroom from the bottom and sides of the pan. When all the wine has evaporated, add the oil and cook the next batch of mushrooms (see page 19). Combine the cooked mushrooms with the onions and garlic in the bowl. Add the mixed herbs, salt and pepper, taste and adjust seasoning.

Melt the remaining 4 tablespoons butter in a small heavy saucepan. Add the flour and make a roux (see page 25) over low heat. Stir often to prevent burning, until the roux is a deep golden brown. Add the stock in a thin stream at first, mixing the roux with the liquid to form a smooth paste. Add the remaining liquid ingredients and bring to a boil. Cook over high heat for 5 to 7 minutes, stirring often. Reduce heat and simmer for about 45 minutes, stirring frequently. If the sauce is not thick enough to coat the back of a spoon, reduce it until you have achieved the desired consistency. Taste and adjust seasoning. Combine the mushrooms and onions with the sauce. Mix well and keep the ragout warm.

Cut the polenta into squares, triangles, diamonds, rectangles or shapes using a cookie cutter. Heat some olive oil in a large skillet, cook the polenta shapes until golden brown. Keep warm in a low heated oven.

To serve: Place polenta shapes on individual plates, spoon the mushroom ragout on top of the polenta, leaving some of the polenta exposed. Garnish with a few slivers of red pepper. Serve immediately. Makes 6 to 8 servings.

Basic Polenta Recipe (page 31)

⅓ pound Parmesan cheese, grated

¼ pound Italian Fontina cheese, grated

2 medium red onions, medium dice

8 cloves garlic, sliced thin

7 Tb. unsalted butter

¾ pound domestic button mushrooms, sliced thick

Handful each of the following wild and cultivated mushrooms: shiitake, Italian field, morel, porcini, oyster, and chanterelle

Olive oil

1 cup red wine, for deglazing

¾ cup fresh mixed herbs (see page 12), heavy on thyme and sage

Salt and pepper, to taste

4 Tb. flour

3 cups strong Mushroom Stock (page 70)

¼ cup port

¼ cup Madeira wine

¼ cup mushroom soy sauce

Garnish: 1 large red pepper, slivered

Risotto Vegetable Timbale
with Tomato Concasse

1 large onion, small dice

4 cloves garlic, minced

¼ pound unsalted butter

1½ cups Arborio rice

5 to 6 cups Basic Vegetable Stock (page 69)

¼ pound Asiago cheese, grated

⅓ pound Italian Fontina cheese, grated

1 large carrot, small dice

½ cup English peas

½ pound asparagus, cut into ¼-inch pieces

1 red pepper, small dice

2 ears sweet corn, shaved

¼ cup minced chives

¼ cup mixed fresh herbs, minced (see page 12)

½ cup fresh basil, chopped

Salt and pepper, to taste

2 whole eggs, lightly beaten

4 Tb. unsalted butter, for timbale molds and parchment

1 cup fine bread crumbs

TOMATO CONCASSE

8 large tomatoes, peeled and seeded

⅓ cup seasoned rice wine vinegar

¼ cup fruity olive oil

Salt and pepper, to taste

Basil sprigs or edible flowers, for garnish

These domes filled with vegetables are stunning. The presentation alone will impress your guests. The recipe is easy and simple to make. Feel free to experiment with different combinations of vegetables.

Cook the onion and garlic in the butter until the onion is soft. Add the rice and cook over high heat for 1 to 2 minutes, stirring constantly. Add 2 cups of the stock and stir, reduce heat and cook over low heat until all the liquid has been absorbed. Add 2 more cups of stock and cook until it is absorbed, finish with the remaining stock. The rice should be tender and creamy at this point. If the rice needs more cooking, add a little more stock and cook until tender. Add the grated cheeses to the risotto and remove from the heat. Cool and set aside.

Blanch the carrots, peas and asparagus separately. Combine the blanched vegetables with the red pepper, corn, and the herbs. When the risotto is cool, add the vegetable mixture. Taste, add salt and pepper and adjust seasoning. Add the eggs to the risotto and mix well.

Preheat oven to 350° F.

Butter 8 to 10 timbale molds or cupcake tins and lightly dust with the bread crumbs. Fill each mold to the top with the rice mixture. Cover the risotto with a small circle of buttered parchment paper to prevent the exposed surface from drying out. Place all the timbale molds in a deep baking pan and fill with hot water to come halfway up the sides of the molds. Bake for 30 to 40 minutes or until the centers are hot.

Meanwhile, cut the tomatoes into small dice, season with the vinegar, oil, salt and pepper. Set aside at room temperature.

When the timbales are done remove from the oven and let sit for 5 to 7 minutes. To unmold, gently tap the bottom and run a knife between the risotto and the sides of the container; invert onto a flat surface. Arrange some of the tomato concasse on each plate, place a timbale on top of the tomato, garnish with a sprig of fresh basil or an edible flower, such as borage, nasturtium, chive blossom, lavender, violet or rose.

Makes about 8 to 10 timbales.

Herbed Ricotta Stuffed Shells
with Tomato Sauce and Pesto

*S*oft, luscious, almost bite-sized pasta shells are pre-sented in a pool of pale red tomato sauce, and drizzled with fresh basil pesto. The ricotta filling, smooth and creamy is rounded out by the lively addition of fresh herbs.

To make the pesto, puree basil, garlic, pine nuts, Parmesan cheese and olive oil in a blender until smooth. To facilitate blending, add a little water. Taste and adjust seasoning. Set aside.

Combine the filling ingredients and mix well. Taste and adjust seasoning.

Cook the pasta shells in a large pot of salted boiling water until just tender. Do not overcook the pasta; the shells must retain their shape so that they can be stuffed. Drain the pasta, and remove any water that has collected in the shells. Pat dry.

Preheat oven to 350° F.

Stuff each shell with the ricotta filling, using a pastry bag, a spoon or your fingers. Bake on greased pie tins or any other baking pan with short sides, for 10 to 15 minutes or until the cheese is soft but not running out. Serve on a pool of tomato sauce and drizzle with the pesto. Garnish with a sprig of parsley or cilantro and serve immediately.

Makes 6 to 8 servings.

PESTO
2 large bunches fresh basil, rough chop
2 cloves garlic, chopped
½ cup pine nuts
½ cup Parmesan cheese, freshly grated
1 cup olive oil
Salt and pepper, to taste

FILLING
2 pounds fresh ricotta cheese
3 cloves garlic, minced
1 large yellow pepper, small dice
1 bunch green onions, minced
⅓ pound Italian Fontina cheese, grated
⅓ pound Asiago cheese, grated
⅓ cup fresh mixed herbs, minced (see page 12)
⅓ cup chives, minced
½ tsp. nutmeg
Salt and pepper, to taste

1 pound large pasta shells
Fresh Tomato Sauce (page 28)
Parsley or cilantro sprigs, for garnish

Antipasto Plate

This exciting combination of sweet and savory, tart and pungent will please even picky eaters. Expand this plate to suit your needs, adding more of your antipasto favorites. The vegetables should be made at least three days before serving, and the caponata is better two or three days after it is made.

Serve this plate with croutons or bread and a fruity olive oil instead of butter.

CAPONATA

2 large yellow onions, medium dice

8 cloves garlic, minced

3 ribs celery, small dice

1 Tb. each dry oregano, basil, thyme and marjoram

1 tsp. red pepper flakes

½ to ⅔ cup fruity olive oil

½ cup red wine

1 large eggplant, medium dice

2 medium zucchini, small dice

½ cup balsamic vinegar

2 cups peeled, seeded and chopped tomatoes

½ cup figs, small chop

2 Tb. sugar

½ cup green olives, pitted

½ cup ripe California olives, pitted

3 Tb. capers

Salt and pepper, to taste

Cook the onions, garlic, celery, herbs and red pepper flakes in the olive oil over high heat for 3 to 4 minutes, stirring frequently. Reduce heat and cook until the onions are soft. Add the red wine and cook over high heat until the wine evaporates. Add the eggplant, zucchini and balsamic vinegar. Cook over moderate heat for 5 to 7 minutes, stirring frequently. Add the tomatoes, figs and sugar and cook over moderately low heat for 30 to 40 minutes or until the eggplant is soft and the mixture is thick. Add the remaining ingredients, cook for 5 more minutes, taste and adjust seasoning.

Makes 4 to 5 cups.

ITALIAN CHEESES

Choose an interesting variety of your favorite Italian cheeses. Think firm and soft, mild and assertive, pungent and plain, blue and spiced. My favorites include Italian Fontina, unaged Asiago, Parmesan Reggiano, tellegio, fresh mozzarella, smoked provolone or mozzarella, Bel Paese, and Gorgonzola.

ASSORTED OLIVES

Choose any *good* assertive olives. Calamata, oil-cured, Niçoise, Gaeta, cracked green, ripe green, Greek or any other similar varieties would be wonderful.

PICKLED VEGETABLES

The vegetables turn a beautiful pastel pink from the raspberry vinegar. These spicy little bites of crisp vegetables are more glamorous and tastier than most pickles.

Blanch separately all the vegetables *except* the onion. Drain, cool and place in a stainless steel or glass bowl with the sliced onion. Bring the remaining ingredients to a boil in a small non-reactive saucepan, reduce heat and cook for 1 minute. Pour the liquid over the cooled vegetables and let sit at room temperature until cool. Store in a glass jar or plastic container in the refrigerator.
    Makes 10 servings.

1 head cauliflower, flowerets only
2 heads fennel, cut into ¼-inch pieces
2 large carrots, 2-inch long roll cut
15 cloves garlic, peeled
1 large red onion, sliced thin
1 cup raspberry vinegar
½ cup seasoned rice wine vinegar
½ cup apple cider vinegar
1 cup sugar
1 Tb. pickling spice
10 whole cloves
10 whole cardamom pods
2 bay leaves
1 tsp. salt
Pinch red pepper flakes

CARAMELIZED ONIONS

I'd have to say onions are one of my favorite foods on earth. In just about any form they're great, but when they are cooked slowly, their natural sugars are released and they turn an irresistible golden brown. If you are like me and can't stop eating these smooth, soft and silky globes, you may want to make a double recipe.

Blanch the onions for 1 minute. Cool, trim the root end and peel, leaving the stem intact. Melt the butter in a heavy skillet, add the onions and cook over high heat, stirring frequently until they turn golden brown. Reduce heat and cook for 20 to 30 minutes. Add the vinegar, wine, salt and pepper and increase the heat. Cook over high heat for 3 to 4 minutes, stirring constantly. When the onions are done, they will be soft, deep brown and sweet. Serve at room temperature or slightly warm.
    Makes 6 to 8 servings.

30 small pearl or boiling onions
3 Tb. unsalted butter
¼ cup balsamic vinegar
Splash of red wine
Salt and pepper, to taste

Fried Cheese
with Corn, Tomato and Pepper Salsa

SALSA

3 ears sweet corn, shaved

1 medium onion, small dice

1 small green pepper, small dice

1 small yellow pepper, small dice

3 to 5 jalapeno peppers, minced

4 large ripe tomatoes, small dice

3 cloves garlic, minced

½ cup cilantro

3 Tb. seasoned rice wine vinegar

3 Tb. olive oil

Salt and pepper, to taste

2 cups fine bread crumbs

1 tsp. each dry oregano, basil, thyme, paprika, sage, black pepper and cumin

1 to 1½ pounds firm cheese, such as Cheddar, Gruyère, mozzarella, provolone, Monterey Jack or havarti

1 cup all-purpose flour

2 eggs, lightly beaten

Vegetable oil, for frying

Even with our "new" health awareness, most people like fried something once in a while. Fried cheese is a heavenly treat . . . crispy, golden brown exterior, with hot oozing cheese inside. What could be better? The perfect companion is the no-fuss zesty salsa. I served this to friends one sunny Sunday afternoon in the backyard. When I returned from the kitchen with my plate seconds later, I found their plates empty. And when I asked, "Do you want more already?" they all nodded their grinning heads in unison. I returned to the kitchen to make a whole new batch.

Combine all the salsa ingredients except the salt and pepper in a large bowl. Season with salt and pepper. Let stand at room temperature for 1 hour, taste and adjust seasoning.

Combine the bread crumbs, spices and herbs. Slice the cheese into pieces ½ inch thick. Dust each piece with flour, dip into the egg, allowing the excess egg to drip off, and coat with seasoned bread crumbs. Set breaded cheese on a sheet pan, and refrigerate for 10 or 15 minutes. When ready to cook, heat about 2 inches of vegetable oil in a large skillet. When oil is hot but not smoking, add the pieces of cheese. *Do not crowd.* Cook over medium-high heat. When one side is golden brown, flip the cheese and cook until the other side is golden brown. Remove cheese from pan and drain on paper towels. Serve immediately, on a bed of the salsa.

Makes 6 to 8 servings.

Cheese Stuffed Chiles
with Corn and Ancho Pepper Sauce

*S*ilky *smooth peppers are filled with luscious melted cheese, served on top of a fiery, dusky ancho pepper sauce and studded with bright kernels of corn. The chiles make a striking presentation.*

Soak the ancho peppers for 2 to 3 hours in water to cover. Remove the seeds and stems.

Roast the red pepper for the sauce and the poblano or green peppers to be stuffed.

To make the sauce: Puree the red pepper, ancho chiles, garlic, balsamic vinegar, maple syrup and chipotle pepper in a blender until smooth. Season with salt and pepper. Taste and adjust seasoning. If the anchos are a little bitter, you can increase the maple syrup. Set aside.

Preheat oven to 350° F.

Carefully peel the roasted poblano or green peppers. Make a small slit down one side of each pepper, big enough to fit the cheese through, but small enough to close and keep the filling inside. Remove all seeds, taking care not to rip the pepper.

To make the filling: Combine the cheeses, garlic, cumin seed and coriander and mix well. Stuff each pepper with the cheese mixture. Pack the cheese in tightly, as it will shrink as it melts. Place stuffed peppers on a greased sheet pan and bake for 15 to 20 minutes or until the cheese is completely melted.

To serve, spoon some ancho sauce onto each plate, sprinkle the corn kernels on top of the sauce, place a stuffed pepper in the middle of the plate and drizzle with crème fraîche. Garnish with a sprig of cilantro.

Makes 6 or 8 servings.

COOK'S NOTE:

When roasting the poblano peppers, do not over char them. Overcooking causes the skin to become very thin, resulting in broken and torn peppers that are difficult to stuff.

SAUCE
6 ancho chile peppers
1 large red bell pepper
2 cloves garlic
3 Tb. balsamic vinegar
2 Tb. maple syrup
1 tsp. chipotle pepper (optional)
Salt and pepper, to taste

FOR STUFFING
6 to 8 poblano, California or green bell peppers

FILLING
¾ pound sharp Cheddar cheese, grated
½ pound Monterey Jack cheese, grated
½ pound smoked cheese, preferably naturally smoked
3 cloves garlic, minced
2 Tb. whole cumin seed
2 Tb. coriander, ground

3 ears white corn, shaved
1 cup crème fraîche or sour cream
Cilantro, for garnish

Vegetable Frittata
with Five-Olive Paste

*T*his could be a delightful brunch offering or a great snack anytime. I like to serve it with the sweet pungent olive paste, but you can choose different sauces or condiments depending on the the mood that strikes you. When sliced, this dish reveals colorful gemlike vegetables in the yellow egg. You can make this early in the day, refrigerate it and serve it later at room temperature.

1 large carrot, small dice

1 large red onion, small dice

1 large red pepper, small dice

1 large green pepper, small dice

1 large zucchini, medium dice

1 tsp. each dry basil, oregano, thyme and chervil

Olive oil

10 eggs, lightly beaten

½ cup half-and-half

¼ pound Parmesan cheese, grated

⅓ pound medium sharp Cheddar cheese, grated

½ cup chives, minced

Salt and pepper, to taste

Watercress or other bitter greens, for garnish

Five-Olive Paste (recipe follows)

Blanch carrots in salted boiling water until tender. Drain and cool. Cook onion, peppers, zucchini and herbs in olive oil until tender, *but not mushy.* Combine the carrots and the sautéed vegetables in a large bowl.

Preheat oven to 350° F.

Combine eggs, half-and-half, cheeses, chives and salt and pepper. Return vegetables to a 12-inch nonstick sauté pan, place over medium heat and add the egg-cheese mixture. Cook over low heat, stirring as if making scrambled eggs. When the eggs are almost set, smooth the top and place the whole pan in the oven. Bake for 30 to 40 minutes or until eggs are set. Remove from the oven. Allow the frittata to sit in the pan for 30 minutes or so at room temperature. When cool, invert onto a large plate. To serve, slice into wedges, garnish with watercress or any other slightly bitter green, such as frisée, escarole, or curly endive. Serve about 2 tablespoons of olive paste with each wedge.

Makes 8 to 10 servings.

FIVE-OLIVE PASTE

Sauté onion, garlic and thyme in the olive oil. When onion is soft, transfer to a food processor, add all the olives, dates and vinegar and process to a fairly smooth paste. Remove from work bowl, taste and adjust seasoning. If you don't have a food processor you can chop the mixture by hand.

Makes 6 to 8 servings.

1 medium red onion, fine chop
3 cloves garlic, minced
2 tsp. dry thyme
⅓ cup fruity olive oil
½ cup Calamata olives, pitted
½ cup oil-cured olives, pitted
⅓ cup Niçoise olives, pitted
¼ cup California ripe black olives, pitted
¼ cup green olives
4 dates, pitted and coarse chop
3 Tb. balsamic vinegar
Black pepper, to taste

Steamed Cabbage Packages
with Hot-Sweet Dipping Sauce

*T*hese cabbage rolls are delicate, fresh and lively. The sweet rice filling is studded with tiny, colorful diced vegetables, subtly flavored with Chinese five-spice powder.

1½ cups basmati rice (see COOK'S NOTE)

1 large carrot, small dice

1 red pepper, small dice

1 bunch green onions, minced

5 cloves garlic, minced

5-inch piece ginger, peeled and minced

1 jalapeno pepper, minced

1 cup roasted cashews, coarse chop

¼ cup sesame oil

3 Tb. soy sauce

½ tsp. Chinese five-spice powder (page 30)

Vegetable oil

4 large eggs, lightly beaten

2 heads Napa or Chinese cabbage

Hot-Sweet Dipping Sauce (recipe follows)

Wash and sort the rice. Cook in 3 quarts of boiling water until tender, 10 to 15 minutes. Drain and set aside. Blanch the carrot. In a large bowl, combine the cooked rice, carrot, red pepper, green onions, garlic, ginger, jalapeno pepper, cashews, sesame oil, soy sauce and five-spice powder. Stir gently with a spoon. Taste and adjust seasoning.

Heat a little oil in a 12-inch pan. Pour in half of the beaten eggs, swirl to the edges and stir until eggs are set, making a thin omelet. Remove from the pan and repeat with remaining egg. Roll each omelet into a long tube and cut across, making very thin strips. Add to the rice mixture and stir in very gently so as not to break the egg ribbons.

Bring a large pot of water to boil. Remove the outer large leaves from the cabbage, taking care not to tear them (See illustration on next page). Cut about one inch of the stem out of each leaf, using a "V" cut. Drop each leaf into the boiling water for 5 to 7 seconds to soften. Drain on lint-free towels. To make stuffing easier and to make bigger rolls, use only the larger leaves. You can use the small ones by placing two together, stem end to stem end, to form a circular shape. These, however, are difficult to roll.

To stuff (see next page), pat the leaves dry, place about 3 tablespoons of filling on the bottom half of a leaf (the cut end). Roll the cabbage leaf around the filling, tucking in the ends, wrapping as tightly as possible. Repeat with other leaves.

To steam rolls, place seam side down on the rack, and steam for 10 to 12 minutes. If you don't have a steamer, place a metal rack in a large pot and fill the pot with water to an inch or so below the rack. The water should not touch the food or the rack. Or you can place the rolls in a skillet with a very small amount of water and cook over low heat, covered, until the rolls are hot. Serve immediately with the sauce. Makes 6 to 8 servings.

HOT-SWEET DIPPING SAUCE

Puree all the ingredients in a blender until smooth. You may need to add more water to aid the blending process, but don't make the sauce too thin. Taste and adjust seasoning.

    Makes 1½ cups.

1 cup black raisins
10 prunes, pitted
2 tomatoes, chopped
½ cup seasoned rice wine vinegar
3 Tb. honey
4 cloves garlic, chopped
1 Tb. red pepper flakes
Pinch cayenne pepper
Splash black vinegar
½ to ⅔ cup water

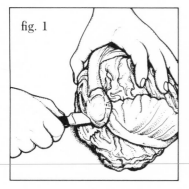

fig. 1

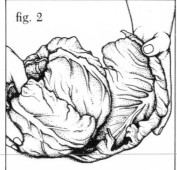

fig. 2

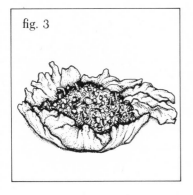

fig. 3

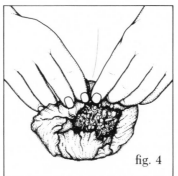

fig. 4

1. Cut core from cabbage.
2. Gently remove outer leaves.
3. Place filling on half of the leaf.
4. Roll the cabbage leaf around the filling, tucking in the ends as you go.

COOK'S NOTE:

Basmati rice is a superior long-grain white rice grown mostly in India, Southeast Asia and Texas. When cooked correctly, the rice is light and delicate, with a slightly sweet taste and nutty aroma. It is delicious on its own; just add a little salt, pepper and butter. Basmati rice is sold at Middle Eastern, Asian, and specialty shops. Some major supermarket chains carry it as well.

Wild Rice Mushroom Fritters
with Port Beurre Rouge

Elegant and rich, these fritters are complex in makeup and flavor. Wild rice provides an almost crunchy texture, while the mushrooms and melted cheese create a tender, soft feel on the tongue. This dish is deep and full of intense flavor.

1 cup wild rice

2 medium onions, small dice

6 cloves garlic, minced

6 Tb. unsalted butter

½ pound button mushrooms, coarse chop

15 medium shiitake mushrooms, sliced thin

¼ cup mushroom soy sauce

Juice from one lemon

1 tsp. each dry thyme, basil, tarragon and sage

¾ cup fresh mixed herbs, minced (see page 12)

5 large egg yolks

6 large egg whites

½ to 1 cup all-purpose flour

½ pound Italian Fontina, grated

¼ pound Asiago cheese, grated

Olive oil

Parsley sprigs, for garnish

Port Beurre Rouge (recipe follows)

Cook the wild rice in 3 quarts of boiling water until it is tender and each grain starts to burst. Drain and set aside.

Cook the onions and garlic in the butter until the onions are soft. Remove from pan and place in a large bowl. In the same pan sauté the button mushrooms over high heat until they are golden brown; add to the onions. Cook the shiitakes in a little butter over low heat until they are soft but not mushy; add to the other mushrooms. Add the mushroom soy, lemon juice, dry and fresh herbs to the mushrooms. Mix well, taste and adjust seasoning.

Lightly beat the egg yolks. Beat the egg whites until stiff, but not dry.

In a small bowl, combine half the mushroom mixture, half the cheeses, half the egg yolks and half the egg whites. Mix gently so as not to break down the egg whites. Add a little flour, enough to form a cohesive batter (see COOK'S NOTE). Stir gently.

Heat some oil in a nonstick skillet. Using about 3 tablespoons of batter for each fritter, carefully spoon the batter into the pan, making small patties. Cook over medium heat until golden brown, flip and cook until other side is golden brown. Keep warm in a low heated oven while you are cooking the remaining fritters. Combine the remaining ingredients and make a another batch of fritters. Be sure the egg whites are still *stiff*. If egg whites have lost some body, simply beat again to form soft peaks.

Serve hot with Port Beurre Rouge. Serve the sauce as a dusky, heady pool beneath the fritters, or drizzle it over them. Garnish with a sprig of parsley.

Makes 6 to 8 servings.

PORT BUERRE ROUGE

Boil the liquid ingredients in a small saucepan over high heat until reduced to about ¼ cup. Reduce the heat and add the butter in pieces, two at a time, stirring all the while. The sauce should be thick, glossy and emulsified. If the sauce separates, remove from the heat and let cool a bit. Add 2 more pieces of unsalted butter, stirring to combine the new butter with the heated butter. Taste and adjust seasoning. You may add an additional splash of balsamic vinegar to perk up the sauce if you like more pungent flavors. Keep the sauce warm over very low heat for not more than 30 or 40 minutes.

Makes 6 to 8 servings.

½ cup red wine
½ cup port
½ cup Madeira
3 Tb. balsamic vinegar
½ pound unsalted
   butter, cut into ½
   inch pieces
Pinch of black pepper

COOK'S NOTE:

Each ingredient plays a significant role in the success of these fritters. The egg yolks provide richness, the whites make the fritters light, flour holds the batter together, cheese is an additional binding, as well as a flavoring agent, and the mushrooms and rice are the base. The juiciness of the mushrooms, dryness of the cheese, stiffness of the egg whites and general condition of the rice all affect the amount of flour to be used. To start, sprinkle flour over the surface of the batter in the bowl so that the flour just covers it. Experiment for the first few fritters, adding flour as necessary.

Spicy Gorditas
with Tomatillo Salsa

*T*hese flavor-packed golden cakes, crunchy on the outside, creamy and seductive on the inside, are so simple and so good they should be outlawed. You won't believe anything so delicious can be so easy to make. One night a good friend, filled from the delights of his own restaurant, tasted one gordita and promptly asked for more. Seven gorditas later, he was stuffed!

5 large baking potatoes, peeled and quartered
1 tsp. salt
1 Tb. coriander, ground
2 tsp. cumin seed, ground
1 tsp. oregano
½ pound sharp Cheddar cheese, grated
1 red pepper, small dice
6 jalapeno peppers, minced
1 cup fresh corn kernels
⅔ cup masa harina flour (see COOK'S NOTE)
1½ tsp. baking powder
Water
Vegetable oil, for frying
Tomatillo Salsa (recipe follows)
Cilantro sprigs, for garnish

Cook potatoes in salted water until they are soft. Drain and mash with a fork or potato masher. Add the spices, cheese, peppers, and corn to the potatoes and mix well. Combine the flour and baking powder, and add to the potatoes a bit at a time, mixing with your hands. Add a little water as you go to make a firm but pliable dough. Set aside.

Take about 3 tablespoons of dough and form a ball, flatten slightly. Make all the dough into balls. Refrigerate the balls for 30 minutes or so. When ready to cook, heat the vegetable oil in a skillet. When oil is hot but not smoking, add the gorditas and cook over medium heat until golden brown on both sides. Spoon some of the salsa onto each individual plate and place 2 or 3 gorditas on top. Garnish with a sprig of cilantro.

Makes 8 to 10 servings.

TOMATILLO SALSA

Cook the tomatillos in salted boiling water until they turn bright green, 1 to 2 minutes. Drain and cool. Puree with all the remaining ingredients in a blender. Taste and adjust seasoning. Serve at room temperature.

Makes about 2 cups.

10 to 15 fresh or 1 large can tomatillos (see COOK'S NOTE)
6 jalapeno peppers, stemmed
4 cloves garlic
1 bunch green onions, chopped medium
1 cup cilantro
Salt and pepper, to taste

COOK'S NOTE:

Masa harina is a flour made from corn. It can be found in Latin American markets. You can substitute *ground* fine cornmeal if masa harina is unavailable.

Tomatillos are small green tomatoes, found in Latin American markets. They have a tart, citrus taste. Fresh tomatillos have a thin paperlike peel that must be removed before cooking. If fresh are unavailable, use canned. Canned tomatillos are already cooked, so you do not need to boil them before pureeing.

Fried Polenta Sandwich

Originally inspired by leftovers, this recipe now stands on its own. This neat package of golden polenta and fresh ricotta is served in a pool of rich tomato sauce. A simple dish to prepare, one that not only holds interest by its good looks, but also by the fabulous tastes and textures. This filling appetizer is the perfect prelude to a lighter entrée. Make the polenta at least 5 hours ahead of serving time to allow it to set properly.

Basic Polenta (page 31)
½ pound Cheddar cheese, grated
¼ pound Parmesan cheese, grated

FILLING
1 pound fresh ricotta cheese
½ pound Italian Fontina cheese, grated
2 red peppers, small dice
3 cloves garlic, minced
¾ cup mixed fresh herbs, minced (page 12)
½ cup green onions, minced
1 tsp. red pepper flakes
Salt and pepper, to taste

Olive oil, for cooking
Tomato Sauce (page 28)
Parsley or cilantro sprigs, for garnish

At least 5 hours before serving, make the polenta, adding the grated Cheddar and Parmesan cheeses just before it is done. Stir well to incorporate the cheeses. Immediately pour polenta into a 9 by 12-inch baking dish and refrigerate for 5 to 6 hours or overnight. When polenta is firm, cut into 3-inch squares. Set aside.

Combine the filling ingredients in a large bowl; taste and adjust seasoning. Place about 2 rounded tablespoons of filling on a polenta square, top with a second square. Repeat using all the squares and filling.

Heat some olive oil in a large nonstick skillet over moderate heat. Cook the polenta sandwiches until golden brown on one side. Carefully turn the sandwiches and cook on the other side until golden brown. Remove from pan and cook the remaining sandwiches. Meanwhile heat the tomato sauce in a saucepan.

Serve the sandwiches on a pool of tomato sauce. Garnish with a sprig of parsley or cilantro.

Makes 6 servings.

Entrées and Meals

These entrées are designed as full meals: The conventional American meal usually consists of a meat, fish or poultry item, starch and a vegetable. Needless to say, the entrées and meals that follow are missing one of those elements! I tried to create a full meal with each entrée so that vegetarian dining doesn't have to be so spartan. Basically, each recipe has a main dish that is served with a side dish or companion dishes. To round out the main course, a salad and some good bread and butter are always welcome.

Vegetable and Cheese Filled Rosti
with Garlic-Shallot Jam

Lively peppers, zucchini, mushrooms and tasty cheeses are sandwiched between two golden brown potato pancakes. Garlic-Shallot Jam is a sweet and soothing taste companion, one that will probably find its way onto your table time and time again.

6 Tb. Olive oil

1 large red pepper, medium dice

1 large zucchini, medium dice

8 cloves garlic, minced

½ pound mushrooms, sliced thick

1 small bunch Swiss chard, cut into 1-inch pieces

2 tsp. dry basil

1 tsp. dry oregano

1 tsp. dry thyme

1 tsp. red pepper flakes

½ pound sharp Cheddar cheese, grated

½ pound Gruyere cheese, grated

6 large boiling potatoes, grated (see COOK'S NOTE)

1 large onion, sliced thin

Salt and pepper, to taste

Vegetable oil, for cooking

Mixed greens, such as frisée, curly endive, escarole, watercress, rocket, radicchio, mustard greens, or mâche, for a bed.

Heat 3 tablespoons olive oil in a large skillet, sauté the red pepper, zucchini and garlic until crisp-tender; set aside in a large bowl. Cook the mushrooms over high heat until golden brown; add to the other vegetables. Cook the chard in 3 tablespoons olive oil until it just wilts; add to the vegetables. Season with herbs and red pepper flakes. When the vegetables are completely cool, add the grated cheese. Taste and adjust seasoning.

In a large bowl, combine the potatoes, onion, salt and pepper. Heat some vegetable oil in a 12-inch nonstick skillet. When the oil is hot but not smoking, add half of the potato-onion mixture. Pat the potatoes down, out to the edges of the pan, to make a large potato pancake. Cook over medium-low heat until the bottom is brown. Slip the pancake out of the pan and onto a large plate, slide it back into the pan, uncooked side down, and cook until golden brown. When potato pancake is done, place on a flat surface and set aside. Repeat the procedure with the remaining potatoes.

Preheat oven to 375° F.

Place one potato pancake in the same 12-inch skillet, spread the filling to the edges, top with the other potato pancake, gently pressing down to seal the pancakes and the filling. Bake for 25 to 30 minutes or until cheese is melted and filling is hot. Remove from the pan by sliding onto a large plate or cutting board. Allow to rest for 5 minutes before cutting into wedges. Serve immediately on a bed of greens with Garlic-Shallot Jam (recipe next page).

COOK'S NOTE:

Use the large side of the grater for the potatoes. If they are grated fine the panckake will be soggy.

GARLIC-SHALLOT JAM

Yes. This is garlic torture. But the result is well worth the effort. If you happen to have children, friends, family or house guests floating about, ask them to peel the garlic.

Separate the cloves of garlic and peel. *Do not smash* the individual cloves in order to peel them; they must remain whole for the jam (see COOK'S NOTE). Cook the onion, garlic and shallots in the butter over high heat until golden brown, stirring constantly. Add the red wine and balsamic vinegar, reduce heat and cook over low heat until liquid has evaporated and garlic is soft. Add the honey, nutmeg, salt and pepper. Taste and adjust seasoning. Serve warm or at room temperature.

Makes 6 to 8 servings.

4 whole heads garlic
1 large onion, medium
    dice
8 shallots, peeled and
    sliced thin
2 Tb. unsalted butter
½ cup red wine
½ cup balsamic vinegar
3 Tb. honey
Pinch of nutmeg
Salt and pepper, to taste

COOK'S NOTE:

To peel the garlic cloves without smashing them, first break all the cloves apart from the stem. Cut the little "nib" off the end of each clove and peel using a paring knife. Some cooks prefer to soak the unpeeled cloves in lukewarm water for about 15 minutes, then peel—but that method leaches some of the flavor out of the garlic.

Eggplant Timbale
with Tomato Sauce
served with Herbed Orzo and Mixed Vegetables with Pine Nuts

T idy little domes of spinach, carrots, mushrooms and savory cheese, all encased in a thin layer of sweet eggplant. Garlic becomes a crunchy golden brown accent to the orzo, and the mixed vegetables are the perfect side dish for the sultry little timbales.

2 large eggplants, sliced into ½-inch thick rounds

Olive oil

Salt and pepper

2 carrots, small dice

2 large onions, small dice

4 cloves garlic, minced

¼ pound unsalted butter

2 bunches spinach, cut into 1-inch pieces

1 pound mushrooms, chopped small

½ pound Italian Fontina cheese, grated

1 tsp. red pepper flakes

1 tsp. thyme

2 tsp. oregano

Salt and pepper, to taste

Tomato Sauce (page 28)

COOK'S NOTE:

Use 1-cup timbale molds or large cupcake tins.

Preheat oven to 350° F.

Brush eggplant slices with some olive oil, sprinkle with some salt and pepper. Bake on sheet pans until eggplant is tender but not mushy, about 10 to 15 minutes. Remove from sheet pans and set aside. Leave oven on.

Blanch carrots and place in a large bowl. Sauté onions and garlic in half of the butter. When onions are soft, add the spinach and cook just until wilted, about 30 seconds. Add to the carrots. In the same skillet, sauté the mushrooms in the remaining butter. Cook over high heat until mushrooms are golden brown. Add to the other vegetables. When vegetables are completely cool, add the remaining ingredients, except the tomato sauce. Taste and adjust seasoning.

"Line" each timbale mold (see COOK'S NOTE) with eggplant, overlapping where necessary to fill any holes. You want a solid lining of eggplant. Fill each mold with the vegetable-cheese mixture, pressing down to pack. Place the molds in a large shallow baking pan. Pour hot water in baking pan to come up three-quarters of the sides of the molds. Bake for 25 to 30 minutes, or until interior is hot. Remove timbales from oven and let rest for 5 minutes. Tap the bottom of each mold, invert onto cutting board.

To serve, spoon some tomato sauce onto each plate, place the timbale on top of tomato sauce and garnish with parsley. Serve with Herbed Orzo and Mixed Vegetables (recipes follow).

Makes 6 to 8 servings.

HERBED ORZO

Cook garlic in 3 tablespoons butter until golden brown and crispy, set aside. Cook orzo in a large pot of lightly salted boiling water until just tender, drain and let cool slightly. Melt remaining 3 tablespoons butter in large pan, add garlic, orzo, herbs, salt and pepper and mix well. Taste and adjust seasoning. Keep warm over very low heat, covered.

Makes 6 to 8 servings.

20 garlic cloves, chopped
6 Tb. unsalted butter
½ to 1 pound Orzo or Riso (rice-shaped pasta)
1 cup mixed fresh herbs, minced (page 12)
Salt and pepper, to taste

MIXED VEGETABLES WITH PINE NUTS

Blanch the broccoli and carrots separately. Heat the oil, add the broccoli, carrots, yellow pepper and garlic and sauté for 1 to 2 minutes. Add the lemon juice, red pepper flakes, salt and pepper. Sauté for 1 more minute and add pine nuts. Serve immediately.

Makes 6 to 8 servings.

2 heads broccoli, flowerets only
2 carrots, julienne
Olive oil
1 medium yellow pepper, julienne
3 cloves garlic
Juice from 2 lemons
Pinch red pepper flakes
Salt and pepper, to taste
⅔ cup pine nuts, toasted

Three-Cheese Lasagne
with Tomato Sauce and Mushroom Port Sauce

*E*ven the most sophisticated gourmet will delight in this combination of smooth and luscious Italian Fontina, nutty Asiago, and sweet ricotta with meaty golden mushrooms and tasty Swiss chard. The flavor-packed square of lasagne rests in a pool of tomato sauce and is then treated to a fine drizzle of rich Mushroom Port Sauce.

CHEESE FILLING

2 pounds fresh ricotta cheese

⅓ pound Asiago cheese, grated

½ pound Italian Fontina cheese, grated

⅓ pound mozzarella cheese, grated

2 large eggs, lightly beaten

6 cloves garlic, minced

¾ cup fresh mixed herbs, minced (page 12)

½ tsp. nutmeg

½ tsp. coriander, ground

Salt and pepper, to taste

MUSHROOM-CHARD FILLLING

1 large onion, medium dice

4 cloves garlic, minced

¼ cup olive oil

1 bunch Swiss chard, cut into 1-inch pieces

½ pound mushrooms, sliced thick

3 Tb. mushroom soy sauce

Black pepper, to taste

Combine ingredients for cheese filling in a bowl, mix well, taste and adjust seasoning. Set aside.

For mushroom-chard filling: Cook onion and garlic in olive oil until onion is soft. Add chopped chard and cook until it wilts, 1 or 2 minutes. Set aside in a bowl and cool. Cook the mushrooms in some olive oil over high heat. When they are golden brown, add the mushroom soy sauce and black pepper. Add to the onion and chard.

To make the béchamel sauce, melt butter in a heavy saucepan, add the flour and cook for 4 to 5 minutes, stirring the roux constantly to prevent burning (see page 25). When the roux has turned a golden brown, add one-third the half-and-half in a slow stream, whisking to make a smooth paste. When mixture becomes a thin paste, add the rest of the half-and-half and the milk. Bring to a boil, reduce heat and cook, stirring often, over moderate heat for 30 to 40 minutes or until sauce is thick. There should be no raw flour taste at this point. If sauce is too thin, continue to cook until it thickens; if it is too thick, add a little more half-and-half or milk. Season with mixed herbs, nutmeg, salt and pepper. Set aside. If there are any lumps, strain through a layer of cheese cloth.

Preheat oven to 350° F.

To assemble, cover bottom of 9 by 13-inch baking pan with a little tomato sauce. Make a layer of pasta sheets over sauce, being sure pasta goes all the way to the edge. Carefully spread half the cheese filling over the pasta, drizzle with a little tomato sauce. Cover with a layer of pasta. Spread the mushroom-chard filling over the pasta, cover with another layer of pasta. Spread the remaining cheese filling over the pasta, cover with the final layer of pasta. Spread all the béchamel sauce over the pasta. Bake for 30 to 35 minutes. *Do not over bake.* Let rest for 5 to 7 minutes, cut into squares and serve on top of the tomato sauce with a drizzle of the Mushroom Port Sauce.

Makes 6 to 8 servings.

BECHAMEL SAUCE
3 Tb. unsalted butter
3 Tb. flour
2 cups half-and-half
¾ cup milk
½ cup mixed fresh
  herbs, minced
  (optional)
Pinch nutmeg
Salt and pepper, to taste

1 to 1½ pounds fresh
  uncooked egg pasta or
  1½ pounds dry
  lasagne ribbons,
  cooked in salted
  boiling water until
  tender
Tomato Sauce (page 28)
Mushroom Port Sauce
  (recipe follows)

MUSHROOM PORT SAUCE

Boil the wine, port and mushroom stock until reduced to about 1 cup, reduce heat and add the butter in small pieces, whisking all the while so that the sauce forms an emulsion. If the sauce seems too thin, boil for 1 to 2 minutes, stirring constantly. Add the black pepper and mushroom soy sauce, taste and adjust seasoning. Keep warm over very low heat.

Makes 6 to 8 servings.

¼ cup red wine
1 cup port
½ cup Mushroom Stock
  (page 70)
4 to 6 Tb. unsalted
  butter
Black pepper, to taste
Splash of mushroom soy
  sauce

Spanish Empanada
with Romesco Sauce
served with Grilled Tomatoes and Onions

FILLING

4 dried ancho chile
   peppers

4 large boiling potatoes,
   medium dice

2 large onions, medium
   dice

8 cloves garlic, minced

2 Tb. cumin seed,
   ground

2 Tb. coriander, ground

2 tsp. red pepper flakes

½ tsp. cinnamon

½ tsp. mace

½ tsp. nutmeg

½ cup fruity olive oil

1 zucchini, medium dice

1 red pepper, medium
   dice

1 green pepper,
   medium dice

½ pound mushrooms,
   sliced thick

1 bunch parsley,
   chopped

6 hard boiled eggs,
   chopped

Salt and pepper, to taste

Empanada Dough
   (recipe follows)

1 cup almonds, coarsley
   ground

2 large eggs, lightly
   beaten

Romesco Sauce (recipe
   follows)

*B*ecause I adore filled things, I've latched onto each and every sample of stuffed pastries. Presented here is the Spanish "pot pie," a tasty, robust and exciting dish. The dough is very easy to make and produces a sturdy but tender crust, golden with the addition of annatto seed. This dough recipe must be doubled, but made in two batches. The tangy Romesco Sauce is a marvelous blend of simple ingredients that makes a fabulous condiment for empanadas. Serve with juicy grilled tomatoes and sweet onions.

Soak ancho chile peppers in water for 2 hours, seed and stem. Puree in blender until smooth.

Cook the potatoes in salted boiling water until tender, but not mushy. Drain and cool.

Cook onions, garlic, and all the spices in the olive oil until the onions are soft. Add the zucchini, red pepper, green pepper and mushrooms. Cook over high heat, stirring often, until the vegetables are tender, but not soft. Add vegetables to the cooled potatoes. Add the ancho pepper puree, parsley and hard boiled eggs. Stir gently so as not to break up the vegetables or eggs. Season with salt and pepper.

Preheat oven to 375° F.

To assemble, divide each ball of dough in half, cut each half into 6 pieces, roll into little balls. With a rolling pin, flatten each ball into a disc, roll out into a 6-inch diameter circle. Sprinkle each round of dough with about 1 tablespoon of ground almonds and place 2 to 3 tablespoons of filling on half of the round. Rub a little water around the edge of the circle, fold the unfilled half over the filling, press the edges together and seal with the tines of a fork. Brush the top with a little beaten egg. Bake on a baking sheet for 30 to 40 minutes, or until crust is golden brown and filling is hot. Serve with Romesco Sauce.

Makes 8 to 10 servings.

EMPANADA DOUGH

Combine the flours and salt in a large bowl. With your hands, mix in the butter. When the butter has been incorporated, add the oil, mixing well with your hands. Add the ice water a little at a time, mixing with your hands until dough forms a ball. Knead for 1 minute, set aside and cover with a damp cloth. Make a second batch of dough in the same manner.

1¾ cups all-purpose flour
¼ cup rye flour
1 Tb. salt
4 Tb. unsalted butter, cut into small pieces
6 Tb. olive oil
6 to 8 Tb. ice water

ROMESCO SAUCE

Puree all the ingredients, except the olive oil and seasoning in a blender. With the motor running, slowly pour in the olive oil, letting the sauce form an emulsion. When all the olive oil has been added, stop the motor, taste and adjust seasoning. Add a little water to aid the blending process and to thin the sauce, if necessary. Add cayenne pepper for a spicier sauce.

Makes about 3 cups.

3 large red peppers, roasted, peeled and seeded
5 cloves garlic
⅓ cup sun-dried tomatoes
⅔ cup blanched almonds
¼ cup balsamic vinegar
Splash of red wine vinegar
⅔ cup fruity olive oil
Salt and pepper, to taste
Cayenne pepper (optional)

GRILLED TOMATOES AND ONIONS

Prepare a charcoal grill.
Cut tomatoes in half. Cut onions in half across the grain.
Brush cut side with olive oil and sprinkle with a generous amount of salt and pepper. Start cooking the onions before the tomatoes, because the onions will take quite a bit longer. Grill over medium-hot coals until onions are soft and tender. Brush periodically with olive oil. Serve immediately.
Makes 6 to 8 servings.

1 small or ½ large tomato per serving
1 small red onion per serving
Fruity olive oil
Salt and Pepper

Assorted Vegetable Cakes
with Grilled Onions and Mustard Butter

*T*hese little golden brown cakes are simple to make. Each one has a unique taste and is matched with unusual and interesting spices and herbs. This is a great winter dish because it calls for many of the winter root vegetables. Serve on a bed of assorted bitter greens with grilled onions and mustard butter.

4 large yellow onions, small dice

5 cloves garlic, minced

4 Tb. unsalted butter

5 large carrots, chopped medium

4 large potatoes, peeled and chopped medium

1 large winter squash, halved and seeds removed

2 celery root, peeled and chopped small

8 large eggs, lightly beaten

12 ounces fine bread crumbs

1 Tb. whole allspice, ground

1 tsp. whole fennel seed

2 tsp. cumin seed, ground

2 tsp. coriander

½ tsp. Five-Pepper Mix (page 29)

Salt and pepper, to taste
  1 cup or more all-purpose flour

Vegetable oil, for frying

Assorted bitter greens: escarole, endive, watercress, curly endive, frisee or mustard greens

Preheat oven to 400° F.

Cook the onions and garlic in the butter until onions are soft. Divide among four medium-sized bowls. Cook the carrots and potatoes separately in salted boiling water until tender, drain and cool. Bake the squash until flesh is soft when pierced with a fork. Remove from oven. When cool remove the flesh from the peel and set aside. Cook the celery root in a little water, covered, until soft. Drain and cool.

Mash each vegetable in a separate bowl with a fork or potato masher. Add one vegetable to each of the four bowls containing the onions. Divide the eggs and bread crumbs equally among the bowls. Mix well. Add the allspice to the squash, fennel to the potatoes, cumin to the carrots, coriander and five-pepper mix to the celery root. Season each with salt and pepper. Taste and adjust seasoning. Refrigerate for 30 to 40 minutes.

Form the vegetables into little cakes, dust with flour and set aside on a sheet pan. Heat vegetable oil in a large nonstick skillet. When oil is hot, but not smoking, add the cakes and cook over moderate heat until golden brown on both sides. Serve immediately on a bed of greens.

Makes 6 to 8 servings.

GRILLED ONIONS AND MUSTARD BUTTER

You may also bake these onions in a 400° F. oven if you do not have a barbeque, but the flavor will be much more interesting if you grill them.

Prepare a charcoal grill.

Blend the butter, mustards, garlic and allspice until smooth. Season with salt and pepper. Keep at room temperature.

Blanch the pearl onions for 1 minute, drain and cool. Remove the outer layer of skin and discard. Trim the root end and just barely trim the stem end. Thread the onions onto wooden skewers (see COOK'S NOTE). Cut the red onions into ¼-inch rounds. Brush all the onions with olive oil, salt and pepper.

Grill the onions over medium-hot coals until they are soft and golden brown. While still hot, brush with copious amounts of mustard butter. Serve immediately.

Makes 6 to 8 servings.

½ pound unsalted butter
3 Tb. coarse-grain mustard
2 Tb. Dijon mustard
2 cloves garlic, minced
½ tsp. whole allspice, ground
Salt and pepper, to taste
20 pearl onions
3 small or medium red onions, peeled
Olive oil

COOK'S NOTE:

Soak the wooden skewers in water for 1 hour to prevent them from burning on the grill.

Savory Roulade
with Herbed Tomato Sauce
served with Potato Pancakes and Sautéed Zucchini

A light and delicate omeletlike pancake is the base for this delicious and rich roulade—perfect for a late morning brunch or an early lunch. The roulade is very good cold the next day, if there is any left.

OMELET

2 Tb. flour

10 eggs, separated and yolks lightly beaten

1 cup half-and-half

1 cup Parmesan cheese, freshly grated

½ tsp. each nutmeg, white pepper and curry powder

Vegetable oil

FILLING

2 onions, small dice

4 cloves garlic, minced

5 Tb. unsalted butter

2 medium green peppers, small dice

½ pound mushrooms, chopped

1 pound fresh ricotta cheese

¼ pound Fontina cheese, grated

¼ pound Gruyère cheese

Pinch red pepper flakes

Salt and pepper

Tomato Sauce (page 28)

1 cup mixed fresh herbs, minced (page 12)

Crème fraîche or sour cream

Parsley or cilantro sprigs, for garnish

Preheat oven to 300° F.

Add the flour to the egg yolks and mix well. Add the half-and-half, cheese and spices and mix well. Beat the egg whites until soft peaks form. Add the yolk mixture to the whites, stirring gently until the mixture is a uniform color. Heat some vegetable oil in a 12-inch nonstick skillet. When the oil is hot, but not smoking, add half the egg mixture. Over low heat, stir the eggs around to the edges of the pan, scraping the bottom as you go, as if you were making scrambled eggs. When eggs are almost set, place pan in preheated oven and bake for 10 to 15 minutes or until eggs are completely set. Remove from the oven and let eggs sit for 10 or 15 minutes in the pan.

To remove from pan, gently nudge the egg from the edges of the skillet, place a large plate over the pancake, flip pan over and invert onto plate. Make another pancake from the remaining batter. Leave the oven on.

Cook onions and garlic in 3 tablespoons of butter until onions are soft. Add the green peppers and cook over high heat, stirring constantly, for 2 to 3 minutes, or until peppers are crisp-tender. Remove vegetables from the pan and set aside in a large bowl. Cook the mushrooms in the remaining butter over high heat until they are golden brown; add to the other vegetables. Combine the ricotta, Fontina, Gruyère and the spices; mix well. When the vegetables are completely cool, combine them with the cheeses, mix well, taste and adjust seasoning.

Spread one half of the filling onto one of the pancakes, leaving a 1-inch border. Roll the roulade as you would a jelly roll, keeping the filling inside. Place seam side down in a shallow baking dish. Repeat using the remaining filling and the other pancake. Heat in the oven for 10 minutes, just to take the chill off.

Make the tomato sauce. Just before serving, add the fresh herbs to the sauce, mix well, taste and adjust seasoning.

To serve, spoon some tomato sauce onto each plate. Slice the roulade into rounds about ½ to ¾ inch thick. Place two rounds on top of the tomato sauce and drizzle with crème fraîche or sour cream thinned with a little water. Garnish with a sprig of parsley or cilantro.

Makes 6 to 8 servings.

POTATO PANCAKES

Squeeze the excess liquid from the potatoes. In a large bowl, combine the potatoes, onion, egg, flour, baking powder, coriander, salt and pepper; mix well. Heat some oil in a large skillet. When the oil is hot, but not smoking, spoon the potato mixture, using 2 tablespoons for each pancake, into the pan. Cook over medium-high heat until golden brown, flip carefully and cook other side until golden brown. Drain on paper towels. Keep the cooked potatoes warm in a low oven, while you cook the remaining pancakes.

Makes 6 to 8 servings.

1½ pounds boiling
    potatoes, grated
1 large yellow onion,
    minced
1 egg, lightly beaten
5 Tb. flour
1 tsp. baking powder
2 tsp. coriander, ground
Salt and pepper, to taste
Vegetable oil, for frying

SAUTEED ZUCCHINI

Sauté zucchini, garlic and red pepper flakes in olive oil until zucchini turns bright green. Add lemon juice, lemon zest, salt and pepper and cook until zucchini is tender and bright green, *not* mushy. Serve immediately.

Makes 6 to 8 servings.

3 zucchini, ¼-inch thick
    diagonal cut
3 cloves garlic, minced
Pinch red pepper flakes
Olive oil
Juice from 1 lemon
Zest from 1 lemon
Salt and pepper, to taste

Spinach Mushroom Filo Roll

served with Preserved Lemon and Tomato-Cucumber Mint Sauté

The presentation alone makes this entrée a winner! There's nothing (well, almost nothing) more seductive than buttery, crisp, filo dough, filled with luscious cheeses and vegetables. The unusual form of this filo concoction makes this dish very special. Tart and sweet lemons are a perfect accompaniment and the Tomato-Cucumber Mint Sauté is refreshing and light. To make the roll, you need to make a filo base, a stack of filo sheets, each buttered and sprinkled with nuts.

FILLING

2 large onions, medium dice

3 cloves garlic, minced

1 Tb. dry basil

2 tsp. dry thyme

2 tsp. dry oregano

Olive oil

1 bunch spinach, coarse chop

¾ pound mushrooms, sliced medium

3 Tb. unsalted butter

1 pound fresh ricotta cheese

⅓ pound Italian Fontina cheese, grated

¼ pound Asiago cheese, grated

3 hard-boiled eggs, chopped

1 carrot, shredded coarse

½ tsp. nutmeg

½ tsp. mace

1 tsp. coriander, ground

Salt and pepper, to taste

1 pound frozen filo dough, thawed (see COOK'S NOTE)

½ pound or more unsalted butter, melted

2 cups finely ground almonds

Parsley sprigs, for garnish

Cook onions, garlic and herbs in some olive oil until onions are soft. Add the chopped spinach and cook over high heat until spinach *just* wilts, about 1 minute. Transfer to a large bowl. Cook mushrooms in the butter over high heat until golden brown; add to the other vegetables. Combine the ricotta, Fontina, Asiago, hard-boiled eggs, carrot, spices, salt and pepper in a bowl; mix well. When the vegetables are completely cool, add the cheese mixture and mix well.

Place one sheet of filo dough on a flat surface (see COOK'S NOTE), brush lightly with some melted butter, sprinkle about 1 tablespoon of ground nuts over the butter, cover with a second sheet of filo dough. Repeat the process, using all the filo dough.

Preheat oven to 350° F.

Gently spread the filling on top of the filo base, leaving a 1-inch border. Roll carefully, keeping the filling on the inside! Brush the roll with butter. Place the roll seam side down in a shallow baking dish and cover loosely with foil. Bake for 30 to 40 minutes, removing the foil after 15 minutes. Let roll rest for 5 to 7 minutes. Cut into slices and serve immediately. Garnish with sprigs of parsley.

Makes about 6 servings.

PRESERVED LEMON

Cut each lemon half into 4 pieces, place with all the remaining ingredients in a nonreactive saucepan and cover with water. Bring to a boil, reduce heat and simmer for 1 hour or until lemons are soft when pierced with a fork. Remove from heat and let sit at room temperature until cool. Store in a covered jar. Serve at room temperature.

Makes 10 servings.

5 whole lemons, halved, pulp removed
1 Tb. Five-Pepper Mix (page 29)
1 Tb. whole allspice
1 tsp. crushed red peppers
1 cup sugar

TOMATO-CUCUMBER MINT SAUTE

Sauté onion and garlic in some olive oil for 1 minute. Add cucumbers and sauté for 1 minute. Add remaining ingredients and sauté for 1 more minute or until tomatoes are juicy. Serve immediately.

Makes 6 servings.

1 medium red onion, sliced thin
2 cloves garlic, minced
Olive oil
2 English cucumbers, peeled, seeded and cut into ¼-inch half moons
1 basket cherry tomatoes, halved
Juice from 1 lemon
Zest from 1 lemon
½ cup pine nuts, toasted
½ cup packed fresh mint, minced
Salt and pepper, to taste

COOK'S NOTE:

Thaw filo dough at room temperature for 2 to 3 hours or in the refrigerator overnight.

Keep the stack of unbuttered filo sheets covered at all times with damp cloth. The sheets dry out very quickly and become impossible to work with. The buttered stack that you are working on will be fine because the top sheet will always have a coating of butter on it.

CREPE BATTER

2 large eggs, lightly beaten

¼ cup corn flour or masa harina (see COOK'S NOTE, page 99)

¾ cup all-purpose flour

1 cup milk

½ cup water

4 Tb. unsalted butter, melted

½ tsp. salt

½ tsp. ground coriander

Pinch nutmeg

Pinch curry powder

Vegetable oil

FILLING

1 medium red onion, small dice

3 Tb. unsalted butter

1 zucchini, small dice

2 ears corn, shaved

½ cup peas, blanched

½ to ¾ pound asparagus, diced and blanched

2 medium avocados, small dice

½ pound Italian Fontina cheese, grated

Salt and pepper, to taste

1 cup crème fraîche or sour cream

½ cup fresh mixed herbs, minced (page 12)

1 pint heavy cream

Summer Vegetable Crepe Packages
with Herbed Crème Fraîche
served with Duo Beet Puree and Cucumber Salad

*D*elicate *corn crepes and fresh summer vegetables team up for a light and seasonal meal. The two beet purees, infused with aromatic spices, make a sparkling condiment for the crepes as well as the cucumber salad.*

Mix the eggs and flours to make a paste. Slowly add the milk, stirring all the while to thin the paste. Add the water, melted butter and spices; mix well. Set aside for 30 minutes.

Heat a little vegetable oil in an 8-inch nonstick skillet. When oil is hot but not smoking, pour in just enough crepe batter to coat the pan. Swirl the batter around to the edges and reduce heat to medium. When edges start to brown and small bubbles appear on the surface of the crepe, flip and cook until just set. (If the crepe is not done on the first side, it will be difficult to flip.) Remove crepe from pan and repeat procedure, using a little oil each time if necessary. The batter should be the consistency of heavy cream, thin with a little milk if necessary. Set all the crepes aside, overlapping one another, covered with plastic or a damp cloth.

Cook the onion in the butter until soft. Add the zucchini and cook until it turns bright green and is crisp-tender. Add the corn and cook for 1 minute. Transfer vegetables to a large bowl. Add the remaining vegetables, mix gently so as not to crush the avocado. Add the cheeses, salt and pepper, mix well, taste and adjust seasoning.

Combine the crème fraîche with the herbs and mix well. Preheat oven to 350° F.

To fill the crepes, place about 2 to 3 tablespoons of filling at the bottom edge of each crepe, tightly roll the crepe around the filling and brush each crepe with heavy cream to prevent them from drying out. Place on greased sheet pans and bake for 15 to 20 minutes or until filling is hot and cheese is melted. Serve immediately with a drizzle of the herbed crème fraîche.

Makes 12 8-inch crepes.

DUO BEET PUREE

Preheat oven to 400° F.

Bake the beets separately in shallow baking dishes with about 1 inch of water. Bake for about 1 hour, or until soft when pierced with a fork. Remove from oven and cool. When cool, peel and trim the root end. Chop coarsely and set aside, red in one bowl, yellow in another.

Cook the apple in 3 tablespoons of butter until soft but not mushy. Add to the red beets and mix well. Add the raspberries, vinegars, spices, salt and pepper; mix well. Puree in a food processor until smooth. If the mixture is too thick, add some water or more vinegar, depending on your taste. Taste and adjust seasoning.

Cook the yellow onion in 3 tablespoons butter until onion is soft. Add the pear and cook until tender. Add this to the yellow beets, along with the remaining ingredients, and mix well. Puree in a food processor until smooth. Taste and adjust seasoning.

Serve about 1 rounded tablespoon of each beet puree per person.

Makes 6 to 8 servings.

3 medium red beets
3 medium yellow beets
2 medium tart green apples, chopped
6 Tb. or more unsalted butter
½ pint raspberries
3 Tb. raspberry vinegar
Splash of balsamic vinegar
Small pinch each ground allspice, nutmeg, mace and clove
Salt and white pepper, to taste
1 small yellow onion, chopped
1 large ripe pear, peeled and chopped
2 Tb. cider vinegar
Splash of sherry vinegar
Small pinch each ground cardamom and coriander

CUCUMBER SALAD

Soak the sliced onion in the rice wine vinegar for 1 hour (see COOK'S NOTE). Drain and discard vinegar.

Combine the cucumbers, carrot and garlic in a bowl.

Place the olive oil in a small bowl, whisk in the vinegars, making an emulsion, season with salt and pepper. Add the onions to the other vegetables and mix. Add the dressing, stir well, taste and adjust seasoning. Serve chilled.

Makes 6 to 8 servings.

1 red onion, sliced thin
½ cup seasoned rice wine vinegar
2 English cucumbers, peeled, seeded and sliced ¼ inch thick
1 large carrot, slivered and blanched
2 cloves garlic, minced

DRESSING
½ cup olive oil
3 Tb. apple cider vinegar
3 Tb. seasoned rice wine vinegar
Salt and pepper, to taste

COOK'S NOTE:

Soaking the onion for the cucumber salad in the vinegar removes some of the bitterness and pungent taste that raw onions sometimes have.

Polenta Shapes
with Chard, Carrots, Sun-Dried Tomatoes and Tomato Cream Sauce

This is one of my favorite dishes. Crispy, golden polenta shapes rest in a pool of rich, creamy tomato sauce and bright green chard. Sweet carrots, and sultry sun-dried tomatoes garnish this stunning and satisfying entrée. Make the polenta early in the day or the day before you plan to serve the dish. The polenta must be firm in order to be shaped and fried.

Basic Polenta (page 31)

⅓ pound Italian Fontina cheese, grated

¼ pound Parmesan cheese, freshly grated

Tomato Sauce (page 28)

1 pint heavy cream

Salt and pepper, to taste

3 carrots, slivered

2 large onions, wedge cut

6 cloves garlic, minced

1 tsp. red pepper flakes

½ cup fruity olive oil

Olive oil, for frying

1 bunch Swiss chard, cut into 1-inch pieces

1 cup sun-dried tomatoes, slivered

COOK'S NOTE:

Once the polenta is fried, the rest of the preparation goes quickly, so have your ingredients ready.

Make the Basic Polenta. Just before it is done, add the Fontina and Parmesan cheeses. Mix well, taste and adjust seasoning. While still hot, pour the polenta into a 9 by 12-inch baking pan, spread evenly to the edges and smooth the top to make an even surface. Refrigerate for 6 hours or overnight.

Make the tomato sauce, add the cream and cook for 5 to 10 minutes. Taste and adjust seasoning. Keep warm over low heat.

Blanch the carrots and set aside. Cook the onions, garlic and red pepper flakes in the fruity olive oil until the onions are soft; set aside in the same pan.

Cut the polenta into squares, rectangles, triangles or fanciful shapes using a cookie cutter. Heat some olive oil in a large skillet. Cook the polenta until golden brown on both sides. Keep warm in a low oven while you prepare the vegetables.

Place the pan with onions over high heat. When hot add the chard, stirring constantly. Cook until chard is bright green and tender. Remove from the heat.

Spoon some tomato sauce onto each plate, top with some chard, place 2 or 3 polenta shapes, depending on the size, on top of the chard, garnish with the carrots and sun-dried tomatoes. Serve immediately.

Makes 6 to 8 servings.

Five-Olive Linguine
with Grilled Vegetables

A very simple dish to prepare, but hardly simple in taste. The sauce is rich with a wild variety of olives, subtly sweetened and tamed by the addition of figs and prunes. Grilled vegetables round out this meal. The dinner can be ready from start to finish in about 1 hour, if the olives are already pitted. Get your coals going while you make the sauce. A light and lively green salad served with a good loaf of warm bread and sweet butter will complete the feast.

Prepare a charcoal grill.

Cook the onions, celery, garlic, herbs and red pepper flakes in the fruity olive oil over low heat until the onions are very soft. Increase the heat, add vinegar and wine and cook over high heat until liquid evaporates. Reduce heat, add prunes, figs, and all the olives; mix well. Cook for 1 to 2 minutes or until heated through. Taste and adjust seasoning.

Cut the squash and eggplant in half lengthwise. Brush all the vegetables with olive oil and sprinkle with salt and pepper. Grill over medium coals until golden brown and juicy. The eggplant will take the longest so put it on first. Tomatoes will take the least amount of time, so grill them last.

Cook the linguine in salted boiling water until al dente. Drain, toss with the olive sauce and serve immediately with the grilled vegetables. Garnish the pasta with minced fresh parsley. I prefer this dish without the usual sprinkling of Parmesan cheese, but you and your guests may have other ideas.

Makes 6 to 8 servings.

3 medium onions, small dice
2 stalks celery, small dice
8 cloves garlic, fine chop
1 Tb. dry thyme
2 tsp. dry oregano
1 tsp. dry sage
1 tsp. red pepper flakes
½ cup fruity olive oil
½ cup balsamic vinegar
¼ cup red wine
8 prunes, pitted and fine chop
½ cup figs, minced
½ cup Calamata olives, pitted and coarse chop
½ cup Niçoise olives, pitted and coarse chop
⅔ cup oil-cured olives, pitted and coarse chop
¾ cup California ripe olives, pitted and coarse chop
½ cup green olives, pitted and coarse chop
Salt and pepper, to taste
Vegetables: Cherry tomatoes, zucchini, yellow squash, Japanese eggplants and scallions (a few pieces per person)
Olive oil, for grilling
Salt and pepper
1½ pounds fresh linguine
Minced fresh parsley, for garnish

Ratatouille Stuffed Tomatoes
with Spinach Linguine

*T*his dish draws from the delights of the Mediterranean, combining assertive, robust tastes—capers, olives, eggplant, tomatoes, garlic and onions. The ratatouille will improve in flavor if made the day before.

RATOUILLE

2 red onions, medium dice

6 cloves garlic, chopped

1 scant Tb. each dry oregano, basil, thyme, marjoram

1 tsp. red pepper flakes

⅔ cup fruity olive oil

1 large eggplant, small dice

⅓ cup balsamic vinegar

⅓ cup red wine

28-ounce can chopped tomatoes in sauce

1 medium zucchini, small dice

1 red pepper, medium dice

1 green pepper, medium dice

½ cup pitted prunes, chopped

½ pound mushrooms, chopped small

2 Tb. unsalted butter

Salt and pepper, to taste

6 to 8 large, firm tomatoes

Cook red onions, garlic, herbs and red pepper flakes in the olive oil until the onions are soft. Add the eggplant, cook over high heat for 1 to 2 minutes, stirring constantly. Add balsamic vinegar and red wine, stir, reduce heat and cook until eggplant is tender but not soft. Add the canned tomatoes, zucchini, peppers and prunes and cook over low heat for 7 to 10 minutes or until vegetables are tender.

Meanwhile, cook the mushrooms in the butter over high heat. When mushrooms are golden brown, remove from the pan and add to the other vegetables. Mixture should be thick and fairly soft. Taste and adjust seasoning. Set aside and cool slightly.

Peel each tomato (see page 17). Cut a ½-inch slice off the top of each tomato. Remove pulp carefully, leaving outer shell intact. Discard pulp or save for stock. Set tomatoes upside down on a flat surface to drain.

To make the pasta, cook yellow onions in the butter and olive oil over high heat for 5 to 7 minutes, stirring constantly. Add the white wine and continue cooking over high heat until the wine evaporates. Reduce heat to low and cook onions until they turn deep golden brown and taste sweet, about 20 to 30 minutes. Turn heat off, but leave the onions in the pan.

Preheat oven to 350° F.

When tomatoes have drained, pat insides dry using a lint-free towel. Fill each shell with the ratatouille, forming a dome at the top. Bake for 30 minutes or until filling is hot.

Meanwhile, add the olives and pine nuts to the onions and heat over a low heat. Cook the pasta in boiling salted water until just tender, 1 minute for fresh or 6 to 8 minutes for dry pasta. Drain well. Add the pasta to the onions, olives and pine nuts and mix well.

When tomatoes are done, heat the pasta quickly, tossing or stirring all the while, add the cheese, remove from the heat and place a generous portion on each plate. Place a tomato in the center of the pasta. Serve immediately. Pass additional cheese.

Makes 6 to 8 servings.

PASTA

3 large yellow onions, ¼-inch wedge cut

3 Tb. unsalted butter

3 Tb. olive oil

½ cup white wine

1 cup oil-cured olives, pitted and coarse chop

¾ cup pine nuts, toasted

1½ to 2 pounds fresh spinach linguine or dry pasta

½ pound Asiago cheese, grated

Salt and pepper, to taste

COOK'S NOTE:

Leftover ratatouille, served at room temperature, with some dark bread, cheese and olives makes a delicious snack.

Pumpkin Ravioli
with Hazelnut Cream and Sorrel Sauce

*H*alloween will never be the same after you indulge in the heavenly flavors of this special and unusual pasta dish. If you have never made your own ravioli before, let this be the first. The satisfaction that comes from making your own filling, forming the packets and then eating them is a true pleasure. The plate will be striking: little nuggets filled with golden pumpkin, creamy white sauce studded with toasty hazelnuts and streamers of bright green sorrel topping the ravioli.

Take note: *this dish requires your undivided attention toward the end, as you time the pasta, reduce the cream and wilt the sorrel. Once the pasta is cooked the sauce must be ready or else the ravioli will get cold, mushy and sticky. The sorrel must not "sit" in the cream sauce or it will turn gray and lose its delicate flavor.*

1 medium pumpkin or 1 large winter squash, halved (or 2½ cups cooked squash)

2 large carrots, chopped and cooked until soft but not mushy

2 yellow onions, small dice

1 clove garlic, minced

2 tsp. coriander

½ tsp. mace

½ tsp. allspice

Pinch cardamom

¼ pound unsalted butter

⅓ pound Parmesan cheese, freshly grated

2 Tb. maple syrup

1 large egg, lightly beaten

Salt and pepper, to taste

1½ pounds fresh egg pasta sheets

Process the cooked pumpkin or squash and carrots in a food processor until smooth.

Cook the onions, garlic and spices in the butter until the onions are soft and golden brown. Add to the pureed vegetables. Add the cheese, maple syrup, egg, salt and pepper. Taste and adjust seasoning. Set aside.

To make the ravioli (see illustrations on next page), lay one pasta sheet out on a flat surface and spray with water to prevent drying and to make the pasta more flexible. Place ½ tablespoon of filling along the bottom edge of the pasta, leaving about a ½-inch space between each dollop. Or, for larger ravioli, use 1 tablespoon of filling and leave 1 inch between dollops. Fold pasta sheet over filling. Use a ravioli cutter to make the edges. Set the finished raviolis aside and cover with a damp cloth.

To make the sauce, cook the cream, garlic, cayenne and pepper over high heat, stirring often. Watch carefully and adjust heat to keep the cream from boiling over. When the cream is thick enough to coat the back of a spoon, add the salt, taste and adjust seasoning. Turn the heat off until ready to use.

Cook the ravioli in salted boiling water until al dente; drain. Reheat the sauce, add the shredded sorrel, cook just until the sorrel wilts, 30 seconds. Add half the hazelnuts and turn the heat off. Add the cooked ravioli, stir gently, serve immediately. Garnish with the remaining hazelnuts.

Makes 6 to 8 servings.

COOK'S NOTE:

Toast hazelnuts in 400° F oven for 10 to 12 minutes or until toasty brown and fragrant. Remove from oven and cool. When cool enough to handle, place in a lint-free towel, wrap tightly and vigorously rub nuts against the towel. Open towel carefully and pick out nuts, discard skins, continue rubbing until nuts are almost blond.

SAUCE

3 cups heavy cream

3 cloves garlic, minced

Pinch each cayenne, white pepper and salt

2 cups sorrel, cut into ⅛-inch strips and stems removed

1 cup hazelnuts, toasted, skinned and slightly crushed (see COOK'S NOTE)

Making Ravioli

1. Place filling along bottom edge of pasta, with ½-inch space between each mound.
2. Fold pasta over.
3. Use a ravioli cutter to make the edges.
4. Set finished ravioli aside, covered with a damp cloth.

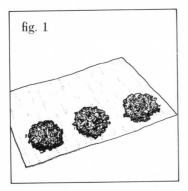

fig. 1

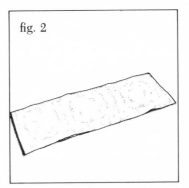

fig. 2

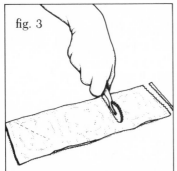

fig. 3

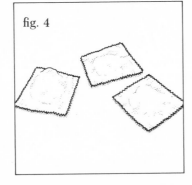

fig. 4

Beet and Spinach Pasta Wheels
with Saffron Cream Sauce

This stunning dish is a unique blend of color, texture and flavor. Even beet haters will be pleased, if not altogether fooled. The presentation alone will impress and delight your guests. I have called for a few extra lasagne noodles to allow for breakage.

4 red beets, cooked and peeled (see COOK'S NOTE)

4 yellow beets, cooked and peeled (see COOK'S NOTE)

3 large onions, small dice

6 cloves garlic, minced

¼ pound unsalted butter

2 bunches spinach, washed and cut into 1-inch pieces

1 Tb. olive oil

1½ pounds fresh ricotta cheese

¼ pound Parmesan cheese, grated

¼ pound Italian Fontina cheese, grated

½ tsp. nutmeg

Salt and pepper, to taste

2 Tb. raspberry vinegar

Pinch each allspice, nutmeg and cinnamon

1 tsp. pure vanilla extract

Pinch each cardamom, coriander and mace

1½ pounds (dry) lasagne noodles with ruffled edges (25 pieces)

Olive oil, for brushing

Puree the red and yellow beets separately in a food processor until smooth. Place each puree in a separate bowl and set aside.

Cook the onions and garlic in the butter until onions are soft and golden brown. Add one third of the onions to the red beets, one third to the yellow beets and place one third in an empty bowl. Set aside.

Cook the spinach in the olive oil until it just wilts and turns bright green. Remove to a colander to cool. With your hands, squeeze out any liquid and add the spinach to the bowl of onions. Add the cheeses, nutmeg, salt and pepper. Mix well. Taste and adjust seasoning.

To the red beets, add the vinegar, allspice, nutmeg, cinnamon and ½ teaspoon vanilla. Mix well, taste and adjust seasoning.

To the yellow beets, add the cardamom, coriander and mace, and the remaining ½ teaspoon vanilla. Mix well, taste and adjust seasoning.

Cook the lasagne noodles in salted boiling water until al dente (see COOK'S NOTE). Drain and carefully rinse with cool water. Immediately lay out on a flat surface, lightly brush both sides of each noodle with a little olive oil and cover with a damp cloth.

Preheat oven to 350° F.

Spread some filling on each noodle, making six of each kind, roll, and place seam side down in a greased shallow baking dish. Bake for 15 minutes, just to warm through.

Meanwhile make the sauce. Cook the cream, garlic, saffron, nutmeg and cayenne in a large wide saucepan over high heat until cream is thick enough to coat the back of a spoon. Add salt and pepper, taste and adjust seasoning.

To serve, spoon some sauce on each plate, place one of each kind of pasta wheel on top of the sauce. Serve immediately. Garnish with a sprig of parsley.

Makes 6 to 8 servings.

SAUCE

3 cups heavy cream

3 cloves garlic, minced

Pinch powdered saffron or a few threads

Pinch each nutmeg and cayenne

Salt and pepper, to taste

Parsley sprigs, for garnish

COOK'S NOTE:

Bake the beets in a shallow baking dish with a little water for 1 hour or more, depending on their size. When cool enough to handle, peel and trim the root and stem.

Cook the noodles in a large roasting pan or a very large kettle so that they have plenty of room to move about. If the water boils too violently, causing the noodle to tear or rip, reduce the heat a little and cook, stirring often, to prevent sticking.

Wild and Domestic Mushroom Risotto
with Madeira Sauce

A luscious, rich and very filling dish that also makes for excellent leftovers. Serve this "meaty" risotto to those with hearty appetites. If imported or wild mushrooms are unavailable, increase the amount of domestic mushrooms. Even without the intense flavors of the imported and wild mushrooms, the risotto will still be quite good.

RISOTTO

2 red onions, medium wedge

6 cloves garlic, minced

¾ pound unsalted butter

½ pound domestic button mushrooms, halved or quartered

½ pound Italian field mushrooms, sliced ¼ inch thick

½ pound porta bella mushrooms, sliced ¼ inch thick

⅓ pound shiitake mushrooms, sliced ½ inch thick

⅓ pound chanterelle mushrooms, sliced into uniform pieces

¼ cup mushroom soy sauce

1½ cups Arborio rice

½ cup red wine

4 to 5 cups Mushroom Stock (page 70)

⅓ pound Parmesan cheese, freshly grated

½ cup fresh mixed herbs, minced (page 12)

Salt and pepper, to taste

1 bunch spinach

Cook the onions and garlic in 4 tablespoons butter until onions are soft; set aside in a large bowl.

Cook each type of mushroom separately; begin with 4 tablespoons butter and add more between batches if necessary (see page 19). Add the mushrooms and mushroom soy to the onions and garlic, mix well and set aside.

Melt 3 tablespoons of butter in a large heavy saucepan, add the rice and cook over moderately high heat for 2 to 3 minutes, stirring constantly. Add the red wine, cook for 1 minute and reduce heat. Add 2 cups of the mushroom stock, stir well and cook over low heat until liquid has been absorbed, 5 to 7 minutes. Add 2 more cups of stock and cook until liquid has been absorbed. Add the remaining stock, cook until saucy and creamy. The rice should be tender at this point. If it needs additional cooking, add a little more stock or water and cook until tender. Remove from heat, add Parmesan cheese and herbs and mix well. Taste and adjust seasoning.

Wash the spinach and dry. Remove the tough stems. Cut the leaves into ⅛-inch ribbons. Set aside.

To make the sauce, cook the Madeira wine, mushroom stock and vinegar in a small saucepan over high heat until reduced to about ⅓ cup. Reduce heat and add the butter in small pieces, stirring constantly. Allow each piece of butter to fully melt before adding the next piece. When all the butter has been used, add the mushroom soy and pepper. Taste and adjust seasoning. The sauce should be the consistency of heavy cream, glossy and rich. Keep warm over low heat.

Add the mushrooms to the risotto and mix well. Heat over low heat until hot, add the spinach, mix in carefully so as not to break the ribbons apart (see COOK'S NOTE). You may need to add a little stock or water at this point to loosen the risotto. Remove the risotto from the heat, place in pasta bowls or on plates and drizzle with the Madeira Sauce. Serve immediately.

Makes 6 to 8 servings.

SAUCE
1 cup Madeira wine
½ cup Mushroom Stock
¼ cup balsamic vinegar
4 Tb. unsalted butter
Splash of mushroom soy sauce
Pepper, to taste

COOK'S NOTE:

The spinach does not need cooking. The heat from the rice and mushrooms alone is enough to properly wilt the fine ribbons, allowing them to retain their bright green color.

Spring Vegetable Risotto
with Grilled Scallions

A rich and creamy rice dish is well balanced with the addition of fresh spring vegetables. A one-bowl supper provides a filling but refreshing, colorful meal.

1 large yellow onion, small dice

6 cloves garlic, minced

¼ pound unsalted butter

2 cups Arborio rice

5 cups Vegetable Stock (page 69)

¾ cup half-and-half

⅓ pound Parmesan cheese, freshly grated

1 cup fresh basil chiffonade (⅛-inch ribbons)

½ cup minced chives

¼ cup fresh mixed herbs, minced (page 12)

Salt and pepper, to taste

3 medium red tomatoes, medium dice

10 small yellow tomatoes, halved

1 pound asparagus, small dice and blanched

2 ears sweet corn, shaved

½ cup peas, blanched

21 scallions, half of the green tops removed

Olive oil, for brushing

Prepare a charcoal grill.

Cook the onion and garlic in the butter over low heat until the onion is soft. Add the rice and cook over high heat for 1 to 2 minutes, stirring constantly. Add 2 cups of the stock, stir, reduce heat and cook until all the liquid has been absorbed. Add 2 more cups of stock and cook until liquid has been absorbed. Add the remaining stock and cook until rice is tender, rich and creamy. Add the half-and-half and remove from the heat. Add cheese, basil, chives, herbs, salt and pepper. Taste and adjust seasoning. The rice should be a little juicy at this point. Set aside.

In a large bowl, combine the tomatoes, blanched asparagus, corn kernels and peas. Add to the rice and gently mix so as not to damage the shape of the tomatoes.

Brush the scallions with some olive oil, sprinkle with salt and pepper. Cook over medium-hot coals until soft and golden brown, 5 to 7 minutes.

Heat the risotto over low heat, stirring often until warm through, taking care not to "smash" the vegetables (see COOK'S NOTE). Serve immediately with the scallions crisscrossed on top of the risotto.

Makes 6 to 8 servings.

COOK'S NOTE:

The cream will make the rice a little liquidy, but the vegetables will absorb some of the cream when you heat the risotto just before serving. The risotto should be creamy and saucy. Do not cook the risotto after the addition of the cream, herbs and vegetables; just heat it.

Eggplant Agrodolci
Red Pepper Fettuccine

Eggplant slices are doused with a sultry reduction of sweet and sour balsamic vinegar. Oil-cured olives, roasted red peppers and toasted pine nuts complete the sauce for this unusual pasta dish. A few heavenly ingredients make for a fabulous and simple meal.

Preheat oven to 400° F.

Brush each slice of eggplant with a generous amount of olive oil, sprinkle with salt and pepper and bake on a sheet pan until eggplant is tender throughout, about 15 minutes.

Meanwhile, boil the vinegar in a small shallow saucepan until reduced to a thick syrupy liquid (see COOK'S NOTE). Remove from the heat. When eggplant is tender but not mushy, remove from the oven and brush both sides of eggplant slices with the vinegar reduction. (If the reduced vinegar starts to thicken or harden, add about 3 tablespoons of new vinegar and heat for 1 minute, stirring constantly.) Cut eggplant into thin strips about 2-inches in length. Set aside.

Cook the onions, garlic, thyme and red pepper flakes in the fruity olive oil over low heat until onions are soft. Cut the red peppers in thin strips and add to the onions. Add the olives, pine nuts and all the eggplant. Mix well and cook for 2 to 3 minutes, add salt and pepper, taste and adjust seasoning.

Cook the pasta in salted boiling water until al dente, about 2 minutes for fresh or 8 to 10 minutes for dry. Drain and add to the sauce. Heat, tossing the ingredients to combine. Serve immediately with grated Parmesan cheese.

Makes 6 to 8 servings.

COOK'S NOTE:

Reducing balsamic vinegar produces a thick and syrupy liquid. Boil the vinegar until it is reduced by at least half, lower the heat a little and watch carefully. The vinegar will turn into a syrup very quickly at this point. If you don't catch it before it goes too far, you will wind up with a thin coating of dark vinegar and a burned pan! If that happens, just wash out the pan and start over.

3 Japanese eggplants or one large American eggplant, sliced into ¼-inch thick rounds

Olive oil, for brushing

Salt and pepper

1½ cups balsamic vinegar

2 medium yellow onions, wedge cut

6 cloves garlic, minced

1 tsp. dry thyme

2 tsp. crushed red pepper flakes

½ cup fruity olive oil

2 large red peppers, roasted, peeled and seeded

1 cup oil-cured olives, pitted and coarse chop

¾ cup pine nuts, toasted

Salt and pepper, to taste

1½ pounds fresh red pepper fettuccine, or any good dry pasta

½ pound Parmesan cheese, freshly grated

Grilled Tofu
with Sesame Buckwheat Noodles and Ginger Mixed Vegetables

A beautifully composed plate with many flavors and colors. Each component is placed on the plate separately, making three little groupings of bright and exciting tastes. The noodles and tofu can be made ahead, held at room temperature for an hour or so, leaving only the vegetables to be sautéed at the last minute.

GRILLED TOFU MARINADE

½ cup peanut oil

½ cup sesame oil

½ cup red wine

¼ cup mushroom soy sauce

¼ cup black vinegar

6 cloves garlic, minced

1 tsp. Chinese five-spice powder (page 30)

4 "blocks" firm tofu

SAUCE

6 green onions, minced

4 cloves garlic, minced

3 Tb. miso, red or white

3-inch piece ginger, peeled and minced

2 jalapeno peppers, minced

½ cup sesame oil

½ cup peanut oil

¼ cup seasoned rice wine vinegar

2 Tb. sherry vinegar

3 Tb. soy sauce

Salt and pepper, to taste

1 cup sesame seeds, toasted

1 to 1½ pounds buckwheat noodles

Combine the marinade ingredients in a large bowl. Add the pieces of tofu and cover with the marinade. Let sit for 6 to 8 hours in the refrigerator or 3 hours at room temperature.

Prepare a charcoal grill.

Remove the tofu from the marinade and drain slightly. Cook over medium-hot red coals, basting frequently with the marinade. "Score" the tofu on both sides making a cross-hatch pattern. Cook until golden brown, about 5 to 8 minutes on each side. Remove from the grill and set aside.

Makes 6 to 8 servings.

SESAME BUCKWHEAT NOODLES

Combine the sauce ingredients in a large bowl. Add half the sesame seeds, mix well. Cook the noodles in salted boiling water until al dente; drain. Add the warm noodles to the sauce, toss and let sit for about 20 minutes. Taste and adjust seasoning.

Makes 6 to 8 servings.

GINGER MIXED VEGETABLES

To prepare the vegetables, sauté the onion and garlic in some peanut oil over high heat until onion is tender, but not soft or translucent. Add the mushrooms, snow peas, and ginger. Cook over high heat, stirring constantly until the mushrooms are tender. Add the broccoli, carrots and sherry, cook for 1 more minute and season with salt and pepper.

To assemble: Cut the tofu into slices about ⅛ inch thick. On each plate, arrange 3 or 4 pieces of tofu overlapping one another. Spoon some of the noodles onto each plate and finish with the vegetables. The tofu and noodles are served at room temperature and the vegetables are served hot. Garnish with a sprig of cilantro.

Makes 6 to 8 servings.

1 yellow onion, wedge cut

2 cloves garlic, sliced thin

⅓ cup peanut oil

6 or 8 shiitake mushrooms, sliced ¼ inch wide

Small handful snow peas, trimmed and strings removed

5-inch piece ginger, peeled and sliced very thin

1 head broccoli, flowerets only, blanched

2 carrots, slivered and blanched

Splash of dry sherry

Salt and pepper, to taste

Cilantro sprigs, for garnish

Eggplant Ravioli
with Tomato, Fennel and Olive Sauce

*S*ighs of ecstasy, moans of contentment and smiling faces will be forthcoming when this pasta dish is served to friends and family. A full-bodied sauce tops savory ravioli filled with eggplant, cheese, herbs and, best of all, sun-dried tomatoes. This is a robust combination of deep and voluptuous flavors. One of my favorites.

RAVIOLI

2 large yellow onions, chopped

6 cloves garlic, minced

1 tsp. dry oregano

2 tsp. dry basil

2 tsp. dry thyme

Pinch cayenne

½ cup fruity olive oil

1 large eggplant, small dice

¼ cup balsamic vinegar

1 cup sun-dried tomatoes, minced

¾ cup fine bread crumbs

½ pound Asiago cheese, finely grated

Salt and pepper, to taste

1 pound fresh spinach pasta, sheets

Cook the onions, garlic, herbs and cayenne in the olive oil until onions are soft; add the eggplant and cook over high heat for 2 to 3 minutes. Add the balsamic vinegar, stir, reduce heat and cook until eggplant is soft but not mushy. Cool slightly. Puree the eggplant in a food processor until smooth, but not liquidy, and place in a large bowl. Add the sun-dried tomatoes, bread crumbs and cheese; mix well. Taste and adjust seasoning.

Make the ravioli according to the directions for Pumpkin Ravioli (see page 122). Set aside, covered with a damp cloth.

Make the tomato sauce.

Cook the onion and garlic in the olive oil until the onion is soft. Add the fennel and cook until just tender. Add all the olives, fennel seed and tomato sauce. Heat thoroughly, taste and adjust seasoning.

Cook the ravioli in salted boiling water until al dente. Drain and place on plates, spoon the sauce over the pasta and serve immediately. Garnish with minced parsley or a sprig of parsley and pass some grated Parmesan.

Makes 6 to 8 servings.

SAUCE

1 recipe Basic Tomato Sauce (page 28)

1 large onion, medium dice

4 cloves garlic, minced

¼ cup olive oil

2 medium or 1 large head fresh fennel, small dice

½ cup Niçoise olives, pitted

⅓ cup oil-cured olives, pitted

¼ cup Calamata olives, pitted

1 Tb. fennel seed, ground

Salt and pepper, to taste

Freshly grated Parmesan cheese, for garnish

Parsley, for garnish

Caramelized Pearls
with Baby Shells

This is my favorite. It takes the last page in the recipe section because I never intended for it to be included .... This was created from humble leftovers, fine ingredients indeed, but nonetheless leftovers. I hope you will be as enchanted as I am with this simple, straightforward pasta dish.

2 pounds pearl onions

¼ pound unsalted butter

2 medium red peppers, small dice

10 cloves garlic, sliced thin

1½ pounds small dry pasta shells

½ cup minced fresh chives

¼ cup fresh herbs, minced

Salt and pepper, to taste

½ pound Reggiano Parmesan cheese, grated (see COOK'S NOTE)

Boil the onions for 1 or 2 minutes, drain and cool. When cool enough to handle, peel and trim the stem end of each onion. Cut the roots if necessary.

Cook the onions in the butter over high heat for 3 to 5 minutes, stirring constantly. When the onions start to brown, reduce heat to low and cook for 30 to 40 minutes or until onions are soft and brown. Add the diced peppers and garlic and cook for 1 minute. Remove from the heat.

Cook the pasta in salted boiling water until al dente, 8 to 10 minutes; drain.

Combine the onions, red peppers and garlic with the pasta in a large pot and heat through. Add the herbs, salt and pepper. Taste and adjust seasoning. When the pasta is hot, serve in large pasta bowls or plates with generous amounts of grated cheese. Dust with freshly cracked black pepper.

Makes 6 to 8 servings.

COOK'S NOTE:

Try to use the best Parmesan cheese you can find. The cheese plays an important role in this simple pasta dish because there are so few ingredients.

Theme Menus

How often have you been grocery shopping and, overwhelmed by the abundance and excellent price of corn or tomatoes, returned home with enough of one vegetable to feed a small country? Better yet, what do you do when the garden explodes with ripe and flavorful vegetables, all ready at once? An entire meal made from one kind of food would be boring at best, but a meal featuring the starring vegetable could be refreshing and challenging. Consider a party where all the guests bring the overflow from their gardens or the local produce market. What could be better than luscious, ripe vegetables bursting with flavor and juice?

Note: All the recipes in the menus can be found in the book by looking up the recipe in the Index.

Vegetable Menus

Corn Picnic

Small Tastes: Tri-Pepper Polenta Squares

Salad: Asparagus and Summer Vegetable Salad

Appetizer: Cheese Stuffed Chiles with Corn and Ancho
Pepper Sauce

Entrée: Summer Vegetable Crepe Packages with Herbed
Crème Fraîche

Eggplant Feast

Salad: Warm Spicy Eggplant Salad with Sesame Noodles

Soup: Spicy Eggplant Soup with Rouille

Entrée: Eggplant Timbale with Tomato Sauce

Onions, Leeks and Garlic Celebration

Small Tastes: Onion Cakes with Spicy Plum Sauce

Soup: Four-Onion and Roasted Garlic Soup

Appetizer: Antipasto Plate

Entrée: Caramelized Pearls with Baby Shells

Tomato Indulgence

Small Tastes: Pear and Cherry Tomatoes with Herbed
Goat Cheese

Salad: Tomato, Date and Fennel Salad

Soup: Tomato Cheddar Cheese Soup

Entrée: Ratatouille Stuffed Tomatoes with Spinach
Linguine

Pepper Banquet

Small Tastes: Roast Pepper Wrapped Hearts of Palm

Soup: Cream of Red Pepper and Tomato Soup

Appetizer: Vegetable Frittata with Five-Olive Paste

Entrée: Savory Roulade with Herbed Tomato Sauce

Potato Party

Small Tastes: Spanish Tortilla with Romesco Sauce

Salad: Warm Grilled Potato Salad

Soup: Coconut Curry Vegetable Soup

Entrée: Vegetable and Cheese Filled Rosti with Garlic-Shallot Jam

Holiday Menus

These holiday menus are based on the produce generally in season. The entrées are full meals on their own, so plan accordingly. If you are cooking for a house full of family or guests, these menus will provide plenty of food!

New Year's Eve

Small Tastes: Roast Pepper Wrapped Hearts of Palm

Salad: Warm Greens with Smoked Mozzarella and Yams

Soup: Wild and Domestic Mushroom Soup with Orzo

Entrée: Pumpkin Ravioli with Hazelnut Cream and Sorrel Sauce

Small Tastes: Chili Roasted Mixed Nuts

Salad: Three-Beet Salad with Pear and Fennel

Soup: Four-Onion and Roasted Garlic Soup

Entrée: Eggplant Agrodolci Red Pepper Fettuccine

New Year's Day

Small Tastes: Imperial Rolls and Curried Samosas with
Fire Dipping Sauce

Salad: Warm Spicy Eggplant Salad with Sesame Noodles

Soup: Coconut Curry Vegetable Soup

Appetizer: Steamed Cabbage Packages with Hot-Sweet
Dipping Sauce

Salad: Warm Red Cabbage Salad

Soup: Tomato Cheddar Cheese Soup

Appetizer: Spicy Gorditas with Tomatillo Salsa

Entrée: Spanish Empanada with Romesco Sauce

Valentine's Day

Salad: Tomato, Date and Fennel Salad

Soup: Cream of Red Pepper and Tomato Soup

Appetizer: Wild Rice and Mushroom Fritters with Port
Beurre Rouge

Entrée: Polenta Shapes with Chard, Carrots, Sun-Dried
Tomatoes and Tomato Cream Sauce

Saint Patrick's Day

Small Tastes: Mushroom Risotto Croquettes

Salad: Romaine with Feta, Figs and Pine Nuts

Entrée: Assorted Vegetable Cakes with Grilled Onions
and Mustard Butter

Passover

Small Tastes: Spinach Mushroom Filo Triangles

Soup: Cream of Summer Squash with Pesto

Appetizer: Fried Cheese with Corn, Tomato and Pepper
Salsa

Entrée: Spring Vegetable Risotto with Grilled Scallions

Easter

Small Tastes: Five-Spice Tea Cooked Eggs

Salad: Asparagus and Summer Vegetable Salad

Soup: Cream of Summer Squash with Pesto

Appetizer: Risotto Vegetable Timbale with Tomato
Concasse

Entrée: Spinach Mushroom Filo Roll

Mother's Day

Small Tastes: Pear and Cherry Tomatoes with Herbed
Goat Cheese

Salad: Asparagus and Summer Vegetable Salad

Soup: Sweet Corn Soup with Chile Pepper

Entrée: Spring Vegetable Risotto with Grilled Scallions

Father's Day

Salad: Warm Grilled Potato Salad

Soup: Cream of Red Pepper and Tomato Soup

Appetizer: Cheese Stuffed Chiles with Corn and Ancho
Pepper Sauce

Entrée: Ratatouille Stuffed Tomatoes with Spinach
Linguine

Rosh Hashanah

Small Tastes: Curried Samosas with Fire Dipping Sauce

Soup: Spicy Eggplant Soup with Rouille

Appetizer: Steamed Cabbage Packages with Hot-Sweet
Dipping Sauce

Entrée: Grilled Tofu with Sesame Buckwheat Noodles
and Ginger Mixed Vegetables

Thanksgiving

Small Tastes: Stuffed Pasta Wheels

Salad: Warm Greens with Smoked Mozzarella and Yams

Soup: Tomato Cheddar Cheese Soup

Appetizer: Wild and Domestic Mushroom Ragout with
Polenta Shapes

Entrée: Eggplant Timbale with Tomato Sauce

Condiments: Cranberry Relish

Chanukah

Small Tastes: Tri-Pepper Polenta Squares

Salad: Tomato, Date and Fennel Salad

Soup: Cauliflower Soup with Melted Gouda Croutons

Appetizer: Eggplant Rollatini with Roasted Red Pepper
Sauce

Entrée: Wild and Domestic Mushroom Risotto with
Madeira Sauce

Christmas

Salad: Three-Beet Salad with Pear and Fennel

Soup: Four-Onion and Roasted Garlic Soup

Appetizer: Antipasto Plate

Entrée: Three-Cheese Lasagne with Tomato Sauce and
Mushroom Port Sauce

Your Birthday

Do not cook. Go out to eat.

Index